A-Z TORBAY

C000293306

CONTENTS

REFERENCE

A Road	A380
B Road	B3195
Dual Carriageway	
One-way Street	
Traffic flow on A roads is also indicated by a heavy line on the drivers' left.	
Under Construction Road	
Opening dates are correct at the time of publication.	
Proposed Road	
Restricted Access	
Pedestrianized Road	
Track / Footpath	
Residential Walkway	
Railway	Heritage Sta. / Station / Level Crossing / Tunnel
Built-up Area	NEW ST.
Beach	
Local Authority Boundary	
National Park Boundary	
Posttown Boundary	
Postcode Boundary (within Posttown)	
Map Continuation	16

Car Park (Selected)	P
Church or Chapel	†
Cycleway (Selected)	
Fire Station	■
Hospital	H
House Numbers (A & B Roads only)	218 17
Information Centre	i
National Grid Reference	290
Park & Ride	Salcombe P+
Police Station	▲
Post Office	★
Safety Camera with Speed Limit	30
Fixed cameras and long term road cameras. Symbols do not indicate camera direction.	
Toilet:	
without facilities for the Disabled	▽
with facilities for the Disabled	▽
Viewpoint	
Educational Establishment	
Hospital or Healthcare Building	
Industrial Building	
Leisure or Recreational Facility	
Place of Interest	
Public Building	
Shopping Centre or Market	
Other Selected Buildings	

SCALE

Map Pages 2-35
1:15,840 4 inches (10.16cm) to 1 mile 6.31cm to 1km

0	¼	½ Mile
0	250	500	750 Metres

Large Scale Inset - Page 30
1:7,920 8 inches (20.32cm) to 1 mile 12.63cm to 1km

0	⅛	¼ Mile
0	100	200	300 Metres

Copyright of Geographers' A-Z Map Company Limited

Fairfield Road, Borough Green, Sevenoaks, Kent TN15 8PP
Telephone: 01732 781000 (Enquiries & Trade Sales)
              01732 783422 (Retail Sales)
www.az.co.uk
Copyright © Geographers' A-Z Map Co. Ltd.
Edition 5 2012

Ordnance Survey This product includes mapping data licensed from Ordnance Survey® with the permission of the Controller of Her Majesty's Stationery Office.

© Crown Copyright 2011. All rights reserved. Licence number 100017302
Safety camera information supplied by www.PocketGPSWorld.com
Speed Camera Location Database Copyright 2011 © PocketGPSWorld.com

Every possible care has been taken to ensure that, to the best of our knowledge, the information contained in this atlas is accurate at the date of publication. However, we cannot warrant that our work is entirely error free and whilst we would be grateful to learn of any inaccuracies, we do not accept any responsibility for loss or damage resulting from reliance on information contained within this publication.

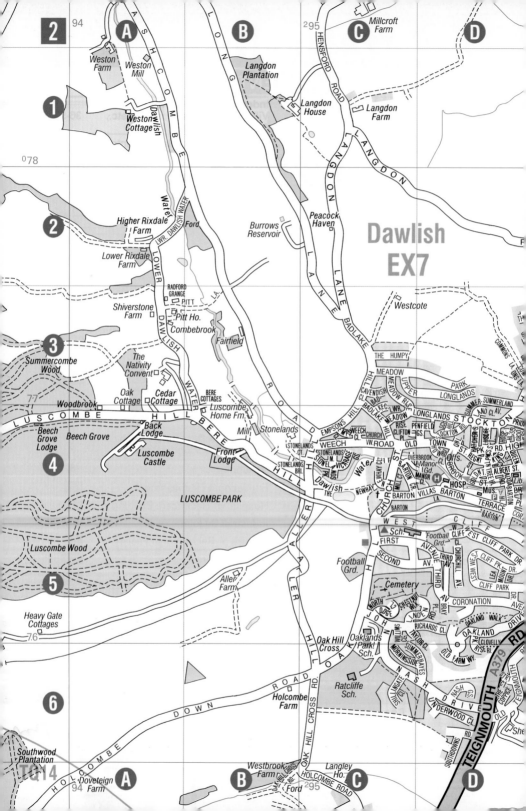

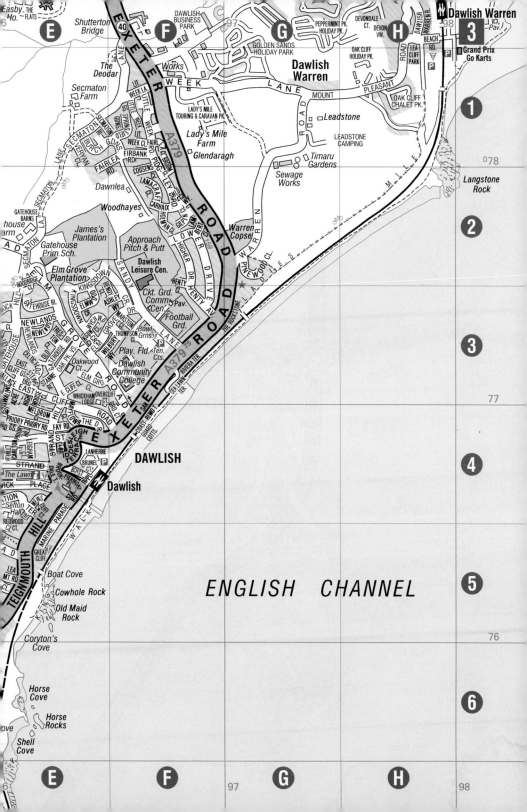

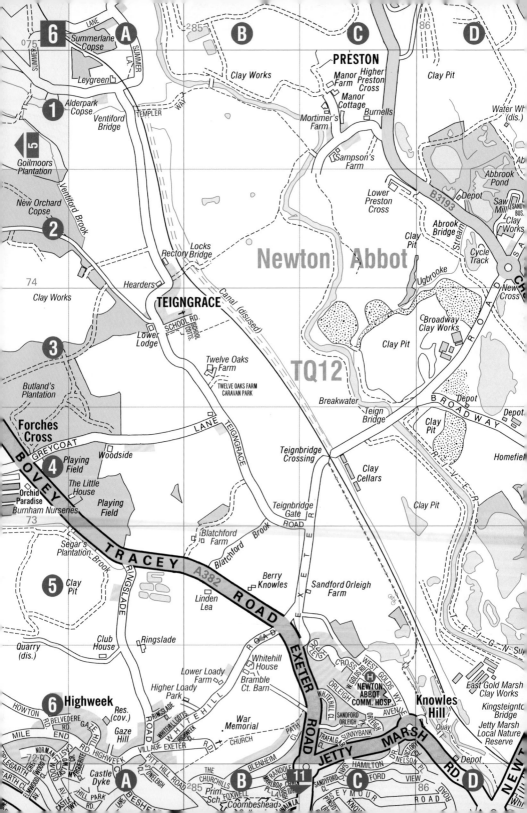

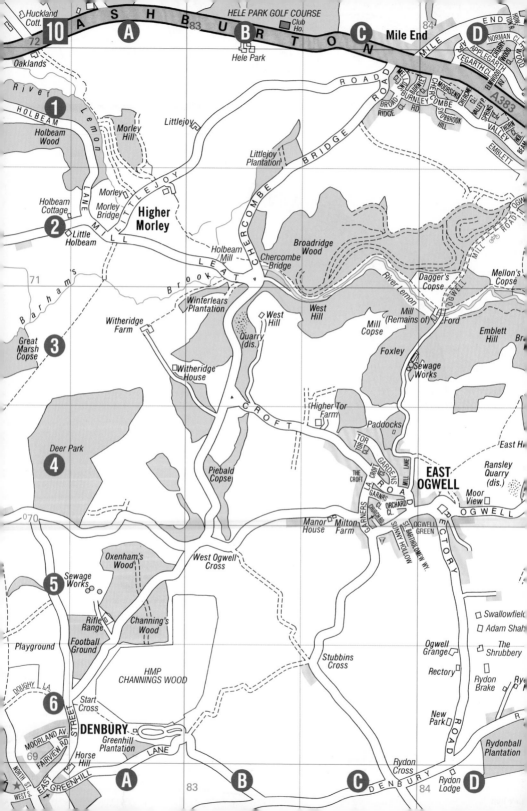

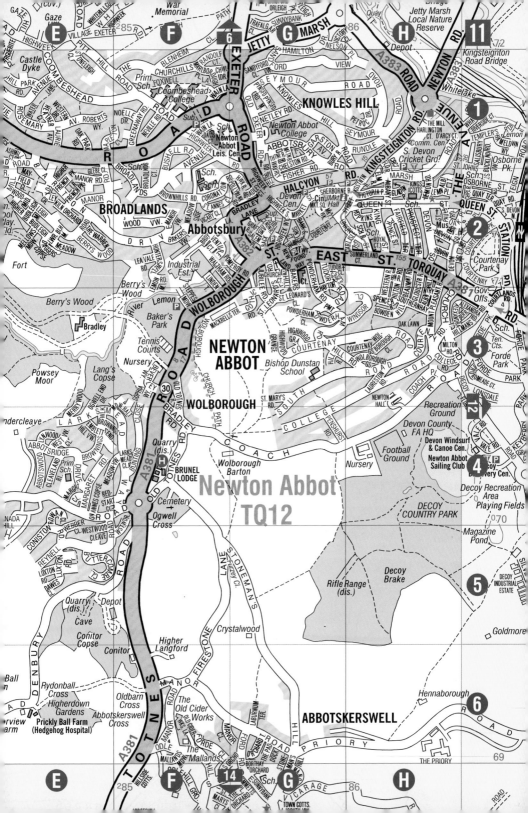

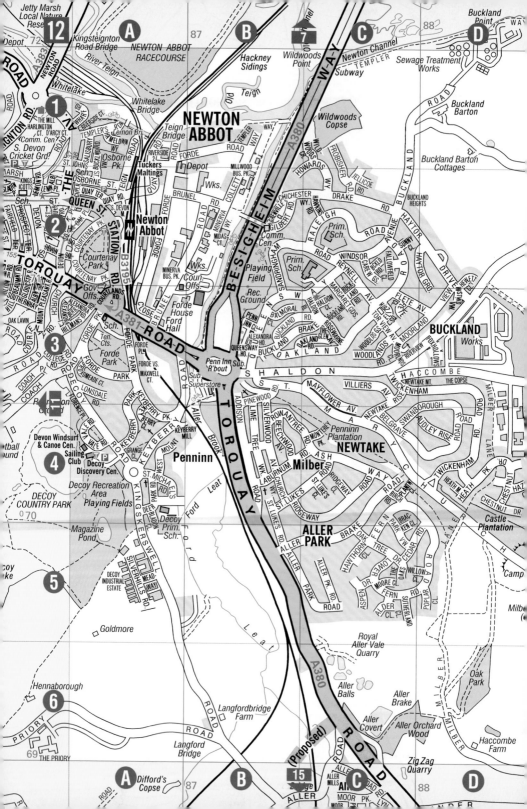

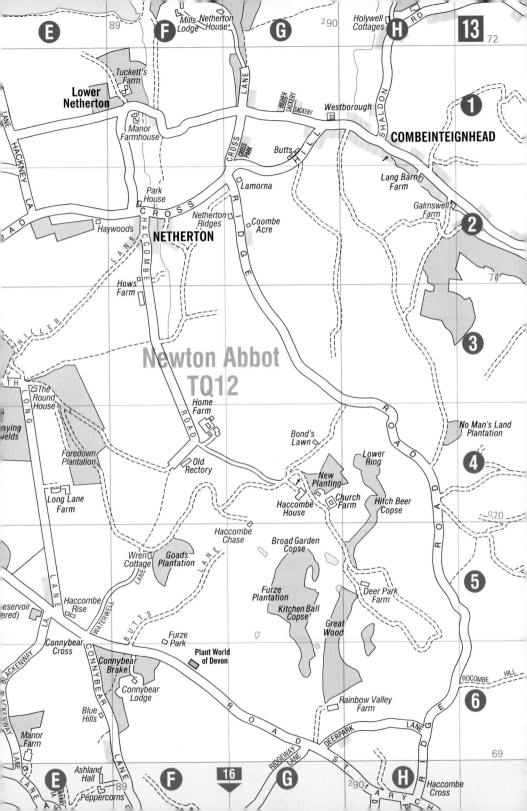

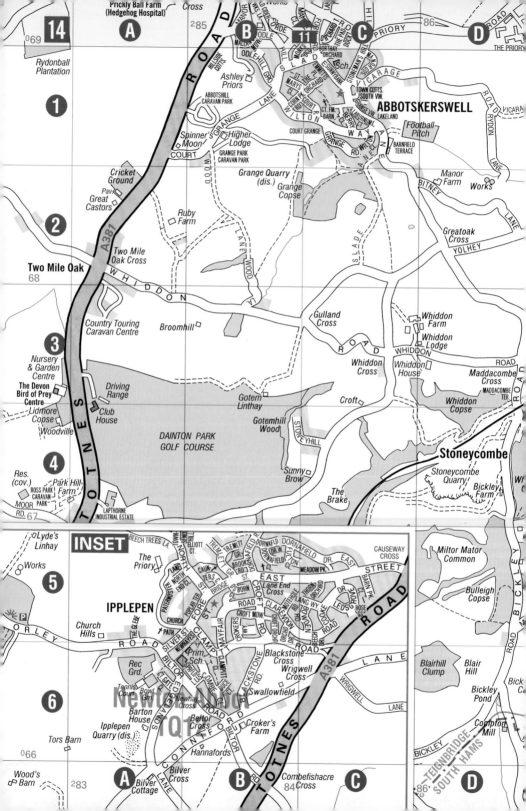

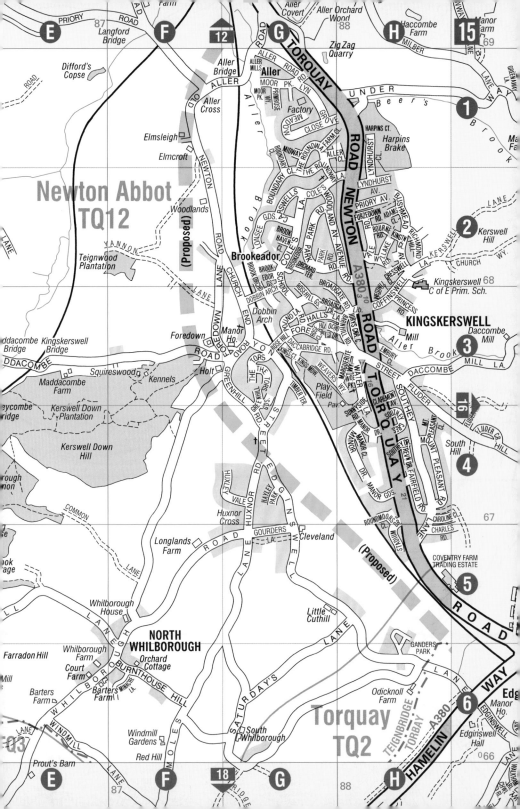

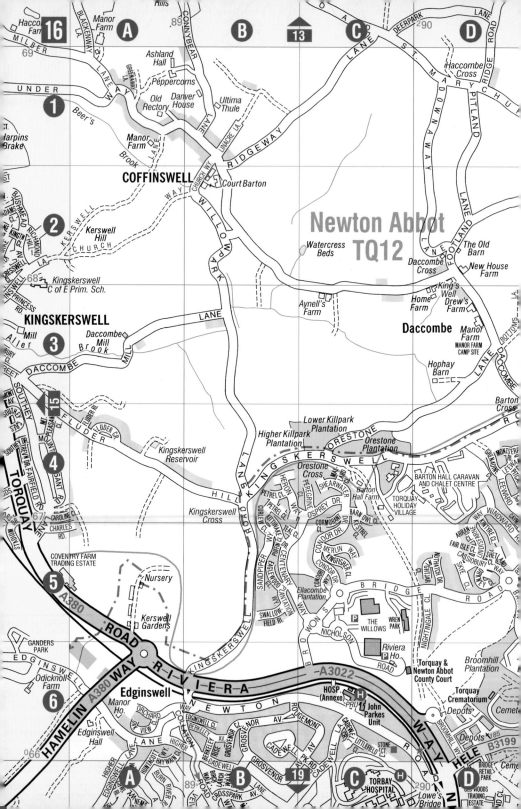

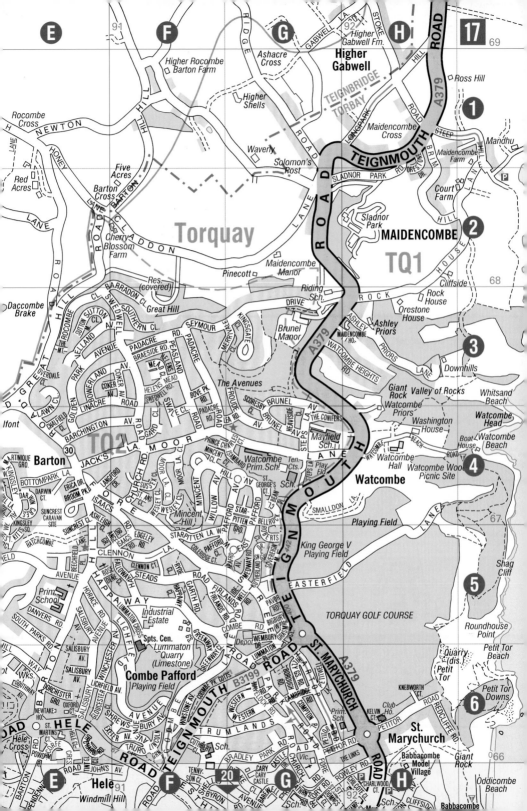

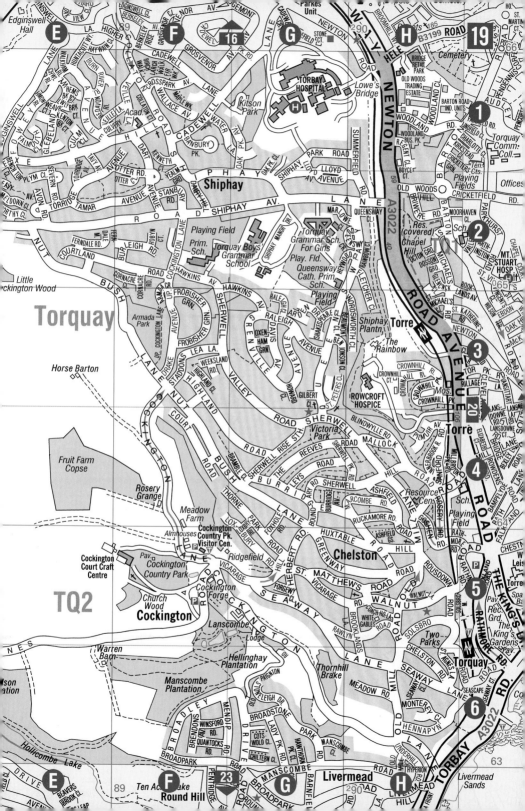

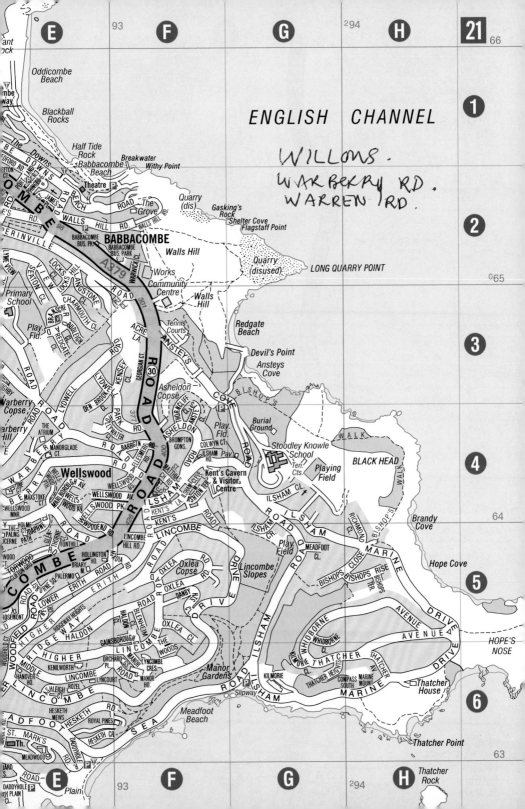

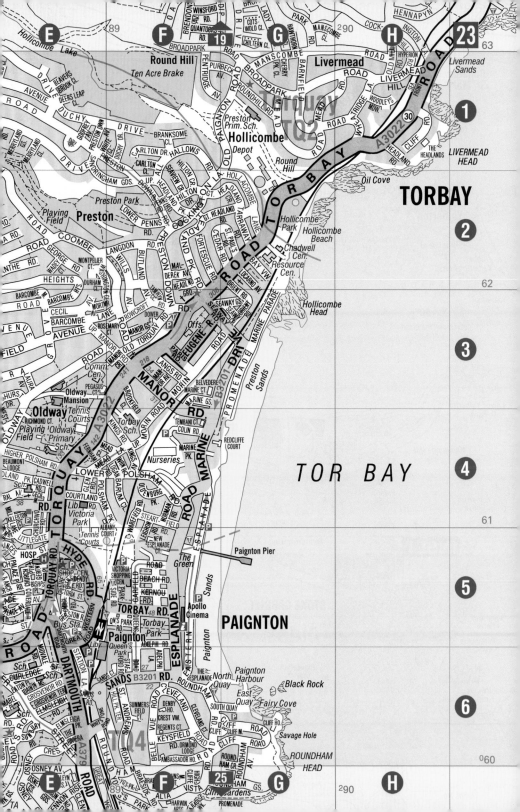

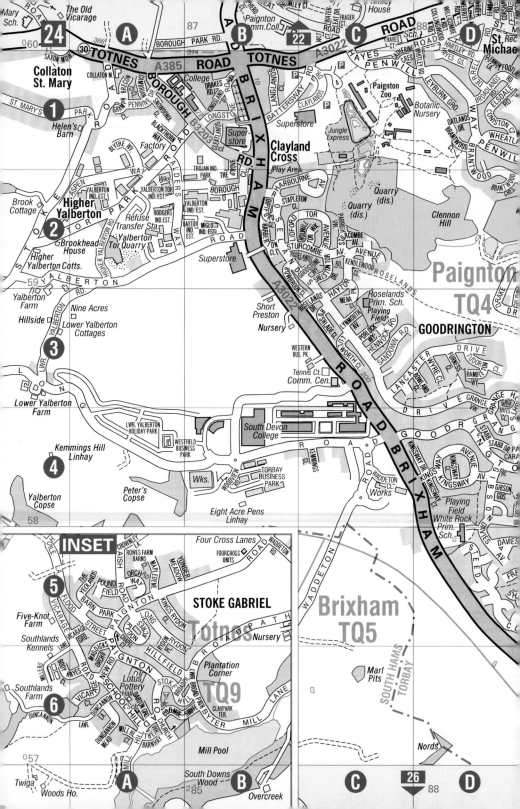

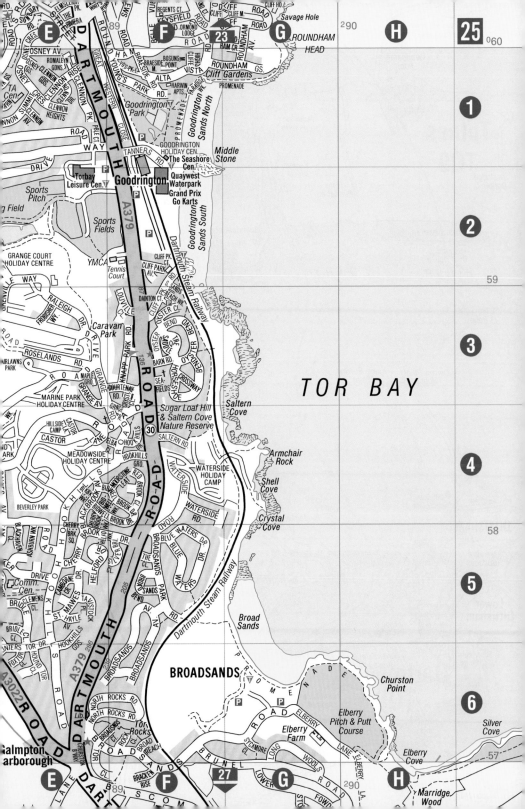

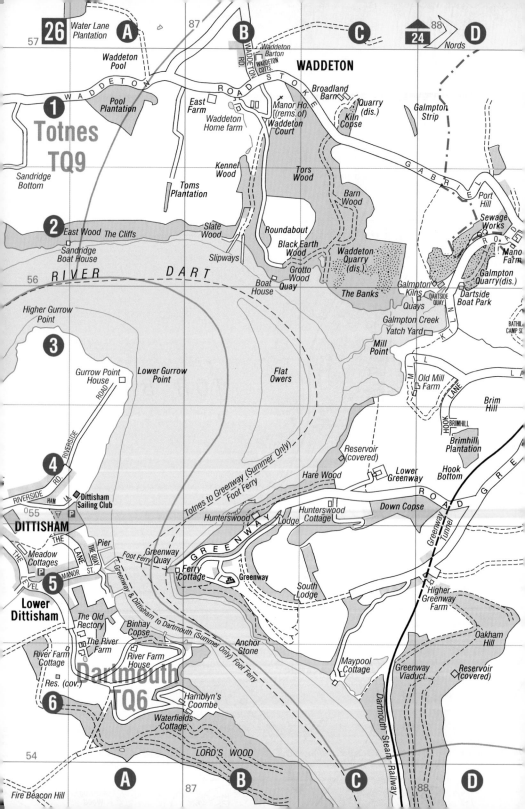

Water Lane Plantation

Waddeton Pool

WADDETON

Waddeton Barton

WADDETON COTTS

①
Totnes TQ9

Pool Plantation

East Farm

Waddeton Home farm

Waddeton Court

Manor Ho. (rems.of)

Broadland Barn

Quarry (dis.)

Kiln Copse

Galmpton Strip

Sandridge Bottom

Kennel Wood

Toms Plantation

Tors Wood

Barn Wood

Port Hill

Sewage Works

GABRIEL

② East Wood The Cliffs

Slate Wood

Roundabout

Black Earth Wood

Waddeton Quarry (dis.)

Mano Farm

Sandridge Boat House

Slipways

Grotto Wood Quay

Boat House

The Banks

Galmpton Kilns

Galmpton Quarry (dis.)

56 R I V E R   D A R T

Dartside Quays

DARTSIDE QUAY

Dartside Boat Park

BATHIL CAMP S

Higher Gurrow Point

Galmpton Creek

Yatch Yard

Mill Point

Old Mill Farm

KILN LANE

Brim Hill

③

Gurrow Point House

Lower Gurrow Point

Flat Owers

MILL LANE

HOOK LANE

BRIMHILL

Brimhill Plantation

RIVERSIDE ROAD

Reservoir (covered)

Lower Greenway

Hook Bottom

④

Hare Wood

ROAD GRE

Totnes to Greenway (Summer Only) Foot Ferry

RIVERSIDE RD.

HAM LA.

Dittisham Sailing Club

055

Hunterswood

Hunterswood Lodge

Hunterswood Cottage

Down Copse

Greenway Tunnel

DITTISHAM

Pier

THE QUAY

THE LANE

MANOR ST.

Foot Ferry

GREENWAY

Greenway Quay

Meadow Cottages

THE LEVEL

⑤

Ferry Cottage

Greenway

South Lodge

Higher Greenway Farm

Lower Dittisham

The Old Rectory

Binhay Copse

Greenway & Dittisham to Dartmouth (Summer Only) Foot Ferry

Oakham Hill

The River Farm

River Farm House

Anchor Stone

Maypool Cottage

Reservoir (covered)

River Farm Cottage

Dartmouth TQ6

Greenway Viaduct

Res. (cov.)

Hamblyn's Coombe

⑥

Waterfields Cottage

Dartmouth Steam Railway

54

Fire Beacon Hill

LORD'S WOOD

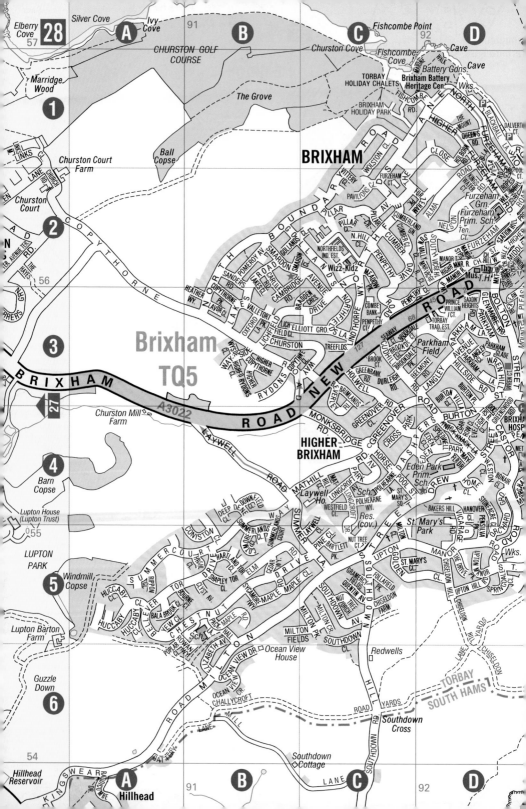

TOR BAY

OUTER HARBOUR

ixham to Torquay Foot Ferry

Brixham Marina

THE BREAKWATER

Jetty
Torbay Lifeboat Station

The Hard

Breakwater Beach

Shoalstone Beach

Shoalstone Pool

Shoalstone Point

Coastguard Station

BREAKWATER CT.

VICTORIA RD.

Ash Hole Cavern

Berry Head Farm

ROAD

Quay

Berry Head Quarry (dis.)

Berry Head Fortifications

Berry Head Lighthouse

1

ixham cht Club

New Fish Quay

New Pier

HARBOUR

Golden Hind

Statue

KING

Outdoor Education Centre

BERRY HEAD

DEVONCOURT

HEATH CT.

RISE

HEATH

SCOTT

WOLBOROUGH GDNS.

Torbay Marina

MARINA CL.

ANCHORAGE

DRIVE

PARK

ROAD

Beacon

BERRY HEAD COUNTRY PARK

Old Redoubt

Visitor Cen.

BERRY HEAD

2

RANSCOMBE

ST.

KINGS REACH

NORTH VIEW

ELKINS HILL

GARLIC

GREAT

LOWER

REA

RD.

GARLIC

RIDGEMAN

WASHBOURNE CL.

HAYCOCK LA.

WALL PARK CL.

WALL

The Bungalow

Beacon

ROAD

Old Redoubt

Picnic Site

56

NC.

MOUNT

WINDMILL

CLOSE

Leisure Centre

Brixham College

Brixham C of E Prim. Sch.

BROAD

LYTE'S

REA

WESTOV

CRES.

FOURVIEW CL.

CENTRY CT.

RANSCOMBE

Playing Field

Astley Park

Swim. Cen.

HILL PK.

HILL PK. CL.

POUNDSGATE RD.

ROAD

Berry Head National Nature Reserve

LANDSCOVE HOLIDAY VILLAGE

Louville Camp

Mew Stone

Cod Rock

3

Durl Head

Durl Rock

BARN

OCHRE

CT.

KINGS

SELLICK

EDINBURGH

CRES.

PENN MEADOWS

MODBURY

ROAD

SEA LANE

Kiln House

GILLARD

MARINA RD.

DOUGLAS

AV.

ST. MARY'S BAY HOLIDAY CENTRE

ST. MARY'S BAY

4

QUEEN'S

HIGHER PENN

WISHINGS

ROAD

ST. MARY'S SHARKHAM

PENN CT.

MARCENT HO.

ST. MARY'S DR.

SHARKHAM DR.

Mussel Rock

055

amping Site

SOUTH BAY HOLIDAY CAMP

SHARKHAM POINT CARAVAN PARK

Mine (dis.)

ROAD

Berry Head National Nature Reserve

Shaft (dis.)

Sharkham Point

Mag Rock

5

own Cliff

ENGLISH CHANNEL

6

54

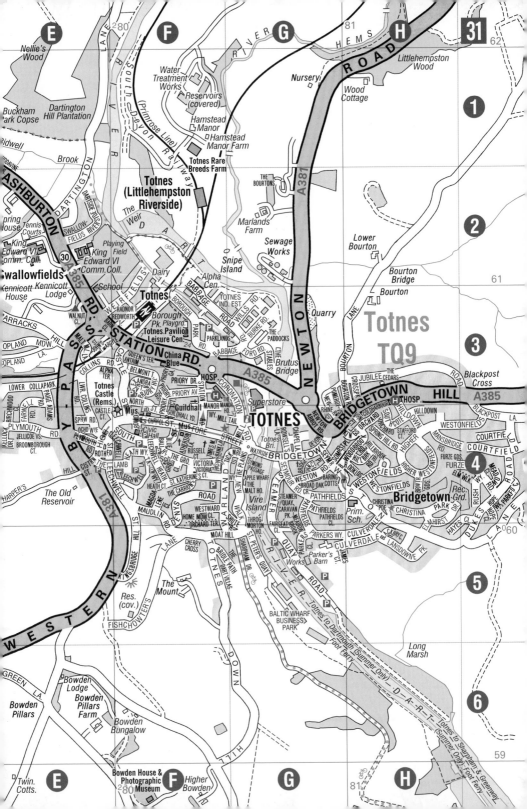

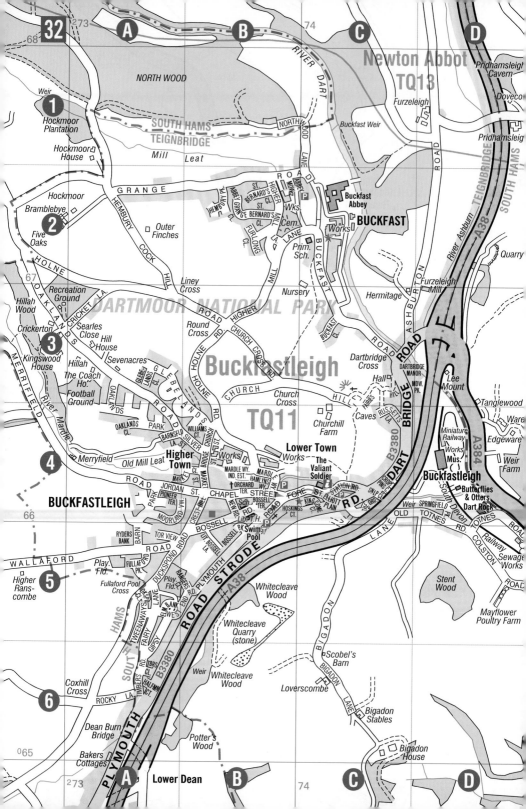

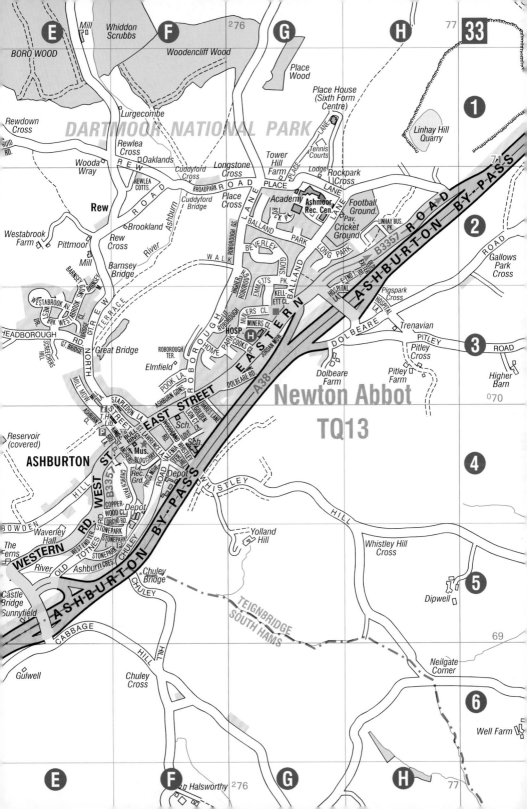

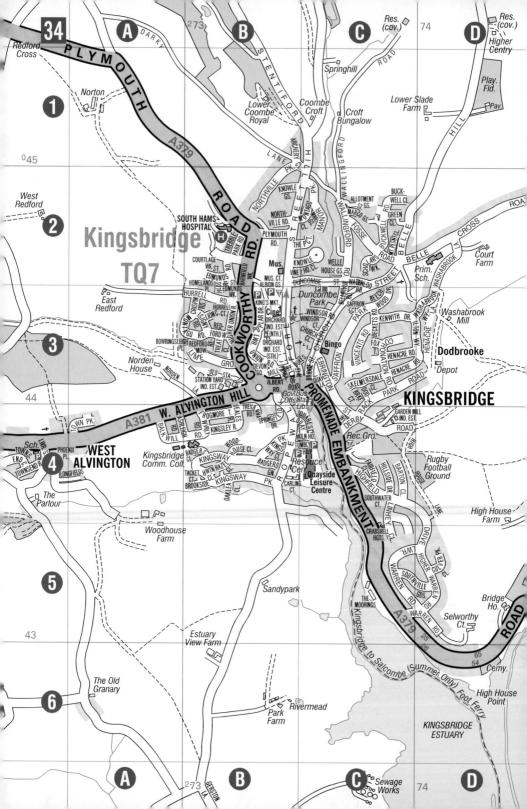

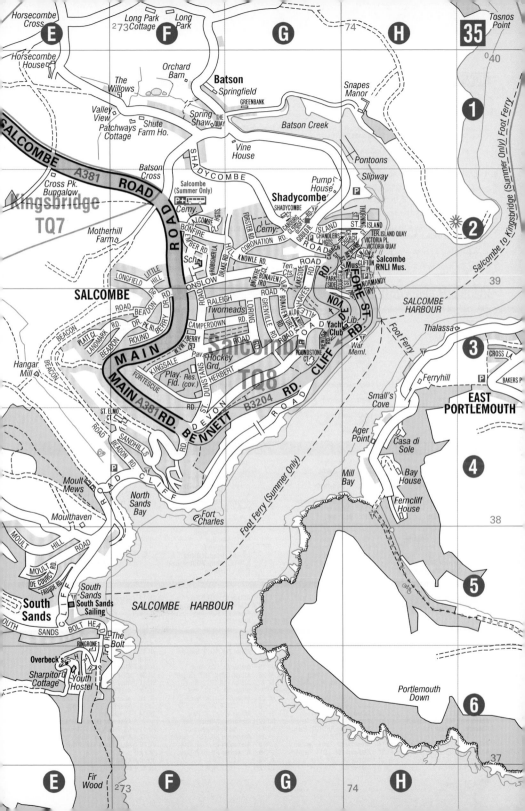

Tosnos Point

E F G 74 H

Horsecombe Cross
Horsecombe House

Long Park Cottage
273
Long Park

°40

1

The Willows
Orchard Barn
Batson
Springfield
GREENBANK
THE QUAY
Spring Shaw

Batson Creek

Snapes Manor

Valley View
Patchways Cottage
Shute Farm Ho.
Cross Pk. Bungalow

SALCOMBE A381 ROAD

Kingsbridge TQ7

Motherhill Farm

Batson Cross

SHADYCOMBE

Vine House

Pontoons

Pump House
P
Slipway

2

Salcombe (Summer Only)
P+
Cemy
Salcombe HGTS.
BONFIRE
EMBER RD.
FORSTER RD.
HOBISH LA.
CORONATION RD.
Cemy
SHADYCOMBE CT.
CARDING CT.
CLIFTON GOULD RD.
ISLAND
THORNING ST.
Island
P
CHANDLERS HGTS.
TER. ISLAND QUAY
VICTORIA PL.
VICTORIA QUAY

39

SALCOMBE

Sch.
ONSLOW
KNOWLE RD.
DRAKE RD.
Ten. Cts.
BRAUNTHE RD.
BONAVENT RD.
LAKESIDE
PARK COURT
Mus.
FORE ST.
CLIFTON PL.
NORMANDY WY.
Salcombe RNLI Mus.

BEACON
LONGFIELD
LITTLE HILL
BEADON RD.
RALEIGH RD.
Tworneads
CAMPERDOWN RD.
BONAVENTURE RD.
GRENVILLE RD.
BONAVEN RD.
HAYES RD.
ALLENHAYES RD.
NEWTON RD.
DEVON RD.
Lib.
SALCOMBE HARBOUR

Thalassa

3

CROSS LA.
BAKERS P.

Hangar Mill

PLATT CL.
LANDMARK
BEADON
ROUND
BERRY DR.
BEADON DR. PK RD.
KINGSALE
FORTESCUE
W.W.
Pav.
Play. Fld.
DUNSTANS RD.
Salcombe TQ8
Hockey Grd.
HERBERT RD.
ST.
POUNDSTONE
Yacht Club
War Meml.
B3204

Small's Cove

Ferryhill

EAST PORTLEMOUTH

Ager Point

Casa di Sole

4

St. ELMO CT.
MAIN A381 RD.
BENNETT RD.
CLIFF ROAD

Mill Bay

Bay House
Ferncliff House

38

SANDHILLS
BEADON RD.
P
Moult Mews

North Sands Bay

Fort Charles

Foot Ferry (Summer Only)

Moulthaven

MOULT HILL ROAD
DE COURCY RD.
FROYDE RD.

5

South Sands
South Sands
South Sands Sailing

SALCOMBE HARBOUR

SOUTH SANDS
BOLT HEAD
RINGRONE
The Bolt

Overbeck's
Sharpitor Cottage
Youth Hostel

Portlemouth Down

6

37

Fir Wood

Including Streets, Places & Areas, Hospitals etc., Industrial Estates,
Selected Flats & Walkways, Stations and Selected Places of Interest.

HOW TO USE THIS INDEX

1. Each street name is followed by its Postcode District, then by its Locality abbreviation(s) and then by its map reference;
   e.g. **Abbey Rd.** TQ2: Torq . . . .4B **20** is in the TQ2 Postcode District and the Torquay Locality and is to be found in square 4B on page **20**.
   The page number is shown in bold type.

2. A strict alphabetical order is followed in which Av., Rd., St., etc. (though abbreviated) are read in full and as part of the street name;
   e.g. **Broad Leaf Pk.** appears after **Broadlands Rd.** but before **Broadley Dr.**

3. Streets and a selection of flats and walkways that cannot be shown on the mapping, appear in the index with the thoroughfare to which they are
   connected shown in brackets; e.g. **Abbeyfield Ho.** *TQ14: Teignm* . . . . *4E 9 (off Heywoods Rd.)*

4. Addresses that are in more than one part are referred to as not continuous.

5. Places and areas are shown in the index in **BLUE TYPE** and the map reference is to the actual map square in which the town centre or area is located and not
   to the place name shown on the map; e.g. **ASHBURTON** 4F **33**

6. An example of a selected place of interest is **Buckfast Abbey** 2C **32**

7. An example of a station is **Dawlish Station (Rail)** . . . .4E **3**, also included is **Park & Ride**
   e.g. **Brixham (Park & Ride)** 2G **27**

8. An example of a Hospital or selected Healthcare facility is **ASHBURTON & BUCKFASTLEIGH COMMUNITY HOSPITAL** 3G **33**

9. Map references for entries that appear on the large scale page **30** are shown first, with small scale map references shown in brackets;
   e.g. **Above Town** TQ6: Dartm 2A **30** (4C **30**)

GENERAL ABBREVIATIONS

App. : Approach	**E.** : East	**Lit.** : Little	**Ri.** : Rise
Arc. : Arcade	**Emb.** : Embankment	**Lwr.** : Lower	**Rd.** : Road
Av. : Avenue	**Ent.** : Enterprise	**Mnr.** : Manor	**Shop.** : Shopping
Bri. : Bridge	**Est.** : Estate	**Mans.** : Mansions	**Sth.** : South
B'way. : Broadway	**Fld.** : Field	**Mkt.** : Market	**Sq.** : Square
Bus. : Business	**Flds.** : Fields	**Mdw.** : Meadow	**St.** : Street
Cvn. : Caravan	**Gdn.** : Garden	**Mdws.** : Meadows	**Ter.** : Terrace
Cen. : Centre	**Gdns.** : Gardens	**M.** : Mews	**Trad.** : Trading
Chu. : Church	**Ga.** : Gate	**Mt.** : Mount	**Up.** : Upper
Cir. : Circus	**Gt.** : Great	**Mus.** : Museum	**Va.** : Vale
Cl. : Close	**Grn.** : Green	**Nth.** : North	**Vw.** : View
Cnr. : Corner	**Gro.** : Grove	**Pde.** : Parade	**Vs.** : Villas
Cotts. : Cottages	**Hgts.** : Heights	**Pk.** : Park	**Vis.** : Visitors
Ct. : Court	**Ho.** : House	**Pas.** : Passage	**Wlk.** : Walk
Cres. : Crescent	**Ind.** : Industrial	**Pl.** : Place	**W.** : West
Cft. : Croft	**Info.** : Information	**Pct.** : Precinct	**Yd.** : Yard
Dr. : Drive	**La.** : Lane	**Prom.** : Promenade	

LOCALITY ABBREVIATIONS

A'well : **Abbotskerswell**	Comp : **Compton**	Holc : **Holcombe**	Pres : **Preston**
Ashb : **Ashburton**	Dacc : **Daccombe**	Ipp : **Ipplepen**	Salc : **Salcombe**
Bat : **Batson**	Darti : **Dartington**	Kingsb : **Kingsbridge**	Shal : **Shaldon**
Bi'ton : **Bishopsteignton**	Dartm : **Dartmouth**	Kingsk : **Kingskerswell**	Sto F : **Stoke Fleming**
Blag : **Blagdon**	Daw : **Dawlish**	Kingst : **Kingsteignton**	Sto G : **Stoke Gabriel**
Bov T : **Bovey Tracey**	Daw W : **Dawlish Warren**	Kingsw : **Kingswear**	S'head : **Stokeinteignhead**
Brixh : **Brixham**	Den : **Denbury**	L'ton : **Littlehempston**	Ston : **Stoneycombe**
Broads : **Broadsands**	Ditt : **Dittisham**	Lwr D : **Lower Dean**	Teigng : **Teigngrace**
Buck : **Buckfast**	E Ogw : **East Ogwell**	Maid : **Maidencombe**	Teignm : **Teignmouth**
B'leigh : **Buckfastleigh**	E Port : **East Portlemouth**	Malb : **Malborough**	Torq : **Torquay**
Chud K : **Chudleigh Knighton**	Galm : **Galmpton**	Marl : **Marldon**	Tot : **Totnes**
Chur F : **Churston Ferrers**	Good : **Goodrington**	Neth : **Netherton**	Two O : **Two Mile Oak**
Coff : **Coffinswell**	Hacc : **Haccombe**	New A : **Newton Abbot**	Wadd : **Waddeton**
Coll M : **Collaton St Mary**	Heat : **Heathfield**	N Whil : **North Whilborough**	W Alv : **West Alvington**
C'head : **Combeinteignhead**	Hill : **Hillhead**	Paig : **Paignton**	

A

Abbey Cl. TQ13: Bov T 3B **4**
  TQ14: Teignm 2E **9**
Abbey Cres. TQ2: Torq 5B **20**
Abbeyfield TQ1: Torq 1C **20**
Abbeyfield Ho. *TQ14: Teignm* 4E **9**
  (off Heywoods Rd.)
Abbey Grange Cl.
  TQ11: Buck 2B **32**
Abbey Mdw. TQ11: Buck 2B **32**
Abbey Pk. 5A **20**
Abbey Rd. TQ2: Torq 4B **20**
  TQ13: Bov T 2B **4**
ABBOTSBURY 2G **11**
Abbotsbury Rd. TQ12: New A . . .1G **11**
Abbotshill Caravan Pk.
  TQ12: A'well 1B **14**
ABBOTSKERSWELL 1C **14**
Abbotsridge Dr. TQ12: E Ogw . . .4E **11**
Abbotswood TQ12: E Ogw 4E **11**
  TQ12: Kingst 3G **7**

Abbrook Av. TQ12: Kingst 2E **7**
Abelia Cl. TQ3: Paig 3B **22**
Above Town
  TQ6: Dartm 2A **30** (4C **30**)
Acacia Cl. TQ12: Kingst 6F **7**
Acland Rd. TQ1: Torq 5F **21**
  TQ8: Salc 3G **35**
Acre La. TQ1: Torq 3F **21**
Addison Rd. TQ4: Paig 6D **22**
  TQ12: New A 3B **12**
Adelphi La. TQ4: Paig 6F **23**
Adelphi Mans. *TQ4: Paig* 6F **23**
  (off Adelphi Rd.)
Adelphi Rd. TQ4: Paig 5F **23**
Admirals Wlk. TQ14: Teignm 1C **8**
Admiral Swimming Cen. 3E **29**
Aircombe Dr. TQ3: Paig 5C **22**
Ailescombe Rd. TQ3: Paig 5C **22**
Aish Rd. TQ9: Sto G 5A **24**
Alandale Cl. TQ14: Teignm 3E **9**
Alandale Rd. TQ14: Teignm 3E **9**
Albany Ct. TQ3: Paig 4E **23**
Albany Rd. TQ3: Pres 2D **22**

Albany St. TQ12: New A 2H **11**
Alberta Cl. TQ14: Teignm 4E **9**
Albert Ct. TQ1: Torq 4C **20**
Albert Pl.
  TQ6: Dartm 1A **30** (4C **30**)
Albert Rd. TQ1: Torq 4C **20**
Albert St. EX7: Daw 4D **2**
Albert Ter. TQ12: New A 2H **11**
  TQ13: Bov T 3B **4**
Albion Ct. TQ5: Brixh 4D **28**
Albion Gdns. TQ7: Kingsb 2B **34**
Albion Hill TQ12: New A 3H **11**
Albion St. TQ1: Shal 6C **8**
Alder Cl. TQ12: New A 5C **12**
  TQ14: Teignm 3D **8**
Alders Way TQ4: Paig 2A **24**
Alexandra Cinema, The
  Scott Cinemas 2G **11**
Alexandra Ho. TQ12: New A 3B **12**
Alexandra La. TQ1: Torq 4C **20**
Alexandra Rd. EX7: Daw 4D **2**
  TQ1: Torq 3C **20**
  TQ12: New A 3A **12**

Alexandra Ter. TQ9: Tot 3F **31**
  TQ12: New A 3H **11**
  TQ14: Teignm 5D **8**
Alfriston Rd. TQ3: Paig 4A **22**
Alison Rd. TQ3: Pres 2D **22**
Allenhayes La. TQ8: Salc 3G **35**
Allenhayes Rd. TQ8: Salc 3G **35**
ALLER 1G **15**
Aller Brake Rd. TQ12: New A 5B **12**
Aller Cl. TQ12: Kingsk 1G **15**
Aller Hill EX7: Daw 5B **2**
Aller Mills TQ12: Kingsk 1G **15**
ALLER PARK 5C **12**
Aller Pk. Rd. TQ12: New A 5B **12**
Aller Rd. TQ12: Kingsk 1F **15**
All Hallows Rd. TQ3: Pres 1F **23**
Allotment Gdns. TQ7: Kingsb . . .2C **34**
All Saint's Rd. TQ1: Torq 3D **20**
Alma Rd. TQ5: Brixh 2D **28**
Alma Steps *TQ6: Kingsw* 5D **30**
  (off Beacon Rd.)
Alpha Ter. TQ9: Tot 3E **31**
Alpine Rd. TQ1: Torq 4C **20**

Bitton Pk. Rd.—Cambrian Cl.

Bitton Pk. Rd. TQ14: Teignm . . . .4C **8** (not continuous)
Blackball La. TQ5: Brixh 1D **28**
Blackberry Cl. TQ9: Tot 5H **31**
Blackberry Way TQ12: Kingst 2F **7**
Blackbrook Av. TQ4: Good 4E **25**
Blackbrook Wlk. TQ4: Good 4E **25**
Blackenway La. TQ12: Coff 6E **13**
Blackhaven Cl. TQ4: Good 5E **25**
Blackpost La. TQ9: Tot 4H **31**
Blackstone Rd. TQ12: Ipp 6B **14**
Blackthorn Way TQ4: Paig 1A **24**
Bladon Cl. TQ12: New A 4A **12**
Blagdon Rd. TQ3: Blag 6A **22**
Blake Cl. TQ1: Torq 1C **20**
Blakey Down La. TQ3: Paig 2B **22**
Blatchcombe Dr. TQ3: Paig 4C **22**
Blatchcombe Rd. TQ3: Paig 4C **22**
Blatchmore La. TQ6: Dartm 5A **30**
Blenheim Cl. TQ1: Torq 5F **21**
TQ12: New A 1F **11**
Blenheim Ter. TQ13: Bov T 3B **4**
Bligh Cl. TQ14: Teignm 1C **8**
Blindwell Av. TQ12: Kingst 4F **7**
Blindwylle Rd. TQ2: Torq 4H **19**
Blogishay La. TQ13: Ashb 4F **33**
Blue Ball Hill TQ9: Tot 4F **31**
Blue Ridge Rd. TQ13: Bov T 6B **4**
Blue Waters Dr. TQ4: Broads . . .5F **25**
Blue Waters Ind. Est.
TQ13: Bov T 5B **4**
Blythe Way TQ4: Paig 1A **24**
Blythswood Cres. TQ1: Torq 2C **20**
Body Hayes Cl. TQ9: Sto G 6A **24**
Bolt Head TQ8: Salc 5E **35**
Bolton Ct. *TQ5: Brixh 3D 28*
(off Windmill Hill)
Bolton St. TQ5: Brixh 3D **28**
Bonair Cl. TQ5: Brixh 4D **28**
Bonaventure Cl. TQ8: Salc 2G **35**
Bonaventure Rd. TQ8: Salc 2G **35**
Bonds Mdw. TQ13: Bov T 2B **4**
Bonfire Hill TQ8: Salc 2F **35**
Boon's La. *TQ7: Kingsb 3B 34*
(off Ropewalk)
Borough Cl. TQ4: Paig 2B **24**
Borough Pk. Rd. TQ3: Paig 6A **22**
TQ9: Tot 3F **31**
Borough Rd. TQ1: Torq 6G **17**
TQ4: Paig 1A **24**
Borthay Orchard
TQ12: A'well 1C **14**
Boscawen Pl. TQ14: Teignm 4D **8**
Bossell Ho. *TQ11: B'leigh 5B 32*
(off Bossell Pk.)
Bossell Pk. TQ11: B'leigh 5B **32**
Bossell Rd. TQ11: B'leigh 5B **32**
Bossell Ter. TQ11: B'leigh 4B **32**
Bosuns Point TQ4: Good 1F **25**
Bottompark La. TQ2: Torq 4E **17**
Bottoms La. TQ12: Dacc 3D **16**
Boundary Cl. TQ12: Kingsk 1G **15**
Boundary Rd. TQ2: Torq 4G **19**
Bourne Ct. TQ5: Brixh 5A **28**
Bourne Rd. TQ12: Kingsk 2H **15**
Bourton La. TQ9: Tot 3G **31**
Bourton Rd. TQ9: Tot 3H **31**
Bourtons, The TQ9: Tot 2G **31**
Bove Pk. Rd. TQ2: Torq 3F **17**
BOVEY TRACEY 3B **4**
Bovey Tracey Golf Course 1A **4**
Bovey Tracey Heritage Cen. 3B **4**
BOVEY TRACEY HOSPITAL 2C **4**
Bovey Tracey Rd.
TQ12: New A 4A **6**
Bowden Hill TQ12: New A 3H **11**
TQ13: Ashb 5E **33**
Bowden House & Photographic Mus.
. . . . .6F **31**
Bowden Rd. TQ12: Ipp 5C **14**
Bowdens Cl. TQ13: Bov T 3B **4**
Bowerland Av. TQ2: Torq 3E **17**
Bowland Cl. TQ4: Paig 3D **24**
Bowling Grn. *TQ13: Ashb 4F 33*
(off Whistley Hill)
Bowringsleigh Pl.
TQ7: Kingsb 3A **34**
Boyce Ct. TQ2: Torq 1H **19**
Boyds Dr. TQ14: Teignm 4E **9**
Bracken Cl. TQ12: New A 4C **12**
Bracken Ri. TQ4: Broads 1F **27**
Bradden Cres. TQ5: Brixh 3B **28**
Braddons Cliffe TQ1: Torq 5C **20**
Braddons Hill Rd. E.
TQ1: Torq 5C **20**
Braddons Hill Rd. W.
TQ1: Torq 5C **20**
Braddons St. TQ1: Torq 5C **20**
BRADLEY 1E **5**
Bradley 3E **11**
Bradley Ct. TQ12: New A 2G **11**
Bradley La. TQ12: New A 2F **11**
Bradley Pk. Rd. TQ1: Torq 1B **20**
Bradley Rd. TQ12: New A 4F **11**
TQ13: Bov T 2D **4**
Braeside M. TQ4: Good 1F **25**
Braeside Rd. TQ2: Torq 3F **17**
TQ4: Good 1F **25**
Brakeridge Cl. TQ5: Chur F 1F **27**
Bramble Cl. TQ2: Torq 4G **19**
Branksome Cl. TQ3: Pres 1F **23**
Branscombe Cl. TQ1: Torq 3E **21**
Brantwood Cl. TQ4: Good 1D **24**
Brantwood Cres. TQ4: Good 2D **24**
Brantwood Dr. TQ4: Good 1D **24**
Breakaway Sports Centre, The
. . . . .6D **20**
Breakneck Hill TQ14: Teignm 1D **8**
Breakwater Ct. TQ5: Brixh 1F **29**
Brecon Cl. TQ4: Coll M 1A **24**
Brendons Av. TQ2: Torq 6F **19**
Brent Rd. TQ3: Paig 5D **22**
Brewery Ct. *EX7: Daw 4E 3*
(off High St.)
Brewery La. *TQ5: Brixh 2D 28*
(off Market St.)
Briary La. TQ1: Torq 4C **20**
Briary M. TQ1: Torq 5E **21**
Bridge Cft. TQ13: Ashb 3E **33**
Bridge Retail Pk. TQ2: Torq 1H **19**
Bridge Rd. TQ2: Torq 4A **20**
TQ5: Chur F 2G **27**
TQ6: Kingsw 1D **30**
TQ14: Shal 6C **8**
Bridge St. TQ7: Kingsb 3C **34**
TQ11: B'leigh 4B **32**
TQ12: Ipp 5B **14**
Bridge St. Ho. *TQ12: New A 2G 11*
(off Bank St.)
BRIDGETOWN 4H **31**
Bridgetown TQ9: Tot 4G **31**
Bridgetown Ct. TQ9: Tot 4G **31**
Bridgetown Hill TQ9: Tot 4G **31**
Bridgewater Gdns. TQ9: Tot 4H **31**
Bridle Cl. TQ4: Good 5E **25**
Bridle Path, The TQ9: Tot 5F **31**
Brim Brook Ct. *TQ2: Torq 1E 19*
(off Chinkwell Ri.)
Brim Hill TQ1: Maid 1H **17**
Brimlands TQ5: Brixh 3C **28**
Brimlands Ct. *TQ5: Brixh 3C 28*
(off New Rd.)
Brimley Bus. Pk. TQ13: Bov T . . .5B **4**
Brimley Ct. TQ13: Bov T 5A **4**
Brimley Cross TQ13: Bov T 5A **4**
Brimley Dr. TQ14: Teignm 4E **9**
Brimley Gdns. TQ13: Bov T 5B **4**
Brimley Grange TQ13: Bov T 5A **4**
Brimley Halt TQ13: Bov T 5B **4**
Brimley La. TQ13: Bov T 5A **4**
Brimley Pk. TQ13: Bov T 5B **4**
Brimley Rd. TQ13: Bov T 5A **4**
Brimley Va. TQ13: Bov T 4B **4**
Briseham Cl. TQ5: Brixh 4E **29**
Briseham Rd. TQ5: Brixh 4E **29**
Britannia Av. TQ6: Dartm 4A **30**
Britannia Mus. 3B **30**
Briwere Rd. TQ1: Torq 2H **19**
BRIXHAM 2E **29**
Brixham (Park & Ride) 2G **27**
Brixham Battery Heritage Cen.
. . . . .1C **28**
Brixham Ent. Est. *TQ5: Brixh . . .3E 29*
(off Windmill Hill)
Brixham Heritage Mus. 2D **28**
Brixham Holiday Pk.
TQ5: Brixh 1C **28**
BRIXHAM HOSPITAL 4D **28**
Brixham Leisure Cen. 3E **29**
Brixham Rd. TQ4: Good, Paig . . .1B **24**
TQ5: Brixh, Chur F 2G **27**
TQ6: Kingsw 4D **30**
Brixham Theatre 2D **28**
Brixham Yacht Club 1E **29**
Broadacre Dr. TQ5: Brixh 2E **29**
Broadgate Cres.
TQ12: Kingsk 3G **15**
Broadgate Rd. TQ12: Kingsk . . .2G **15**
BROADLANDS 2E **11**
Broadlands TQ14: Shal 6C **8**
Broadlands Av. TQ12: New A . . .2F **11**
Broadlands Ct. TQ12: New A . . .2F **11**
Broadlands Rd. TQ4: Paig 1D **24**
Broad Leaf Pk. TQ14: Teignm 2G **9**
Broadley Dr. TQ2: Torq 6F **19**
Broadmeade Ct.
TQ12: New A 3A **12**
Broadmeadow Ind. Est.
TQ14: Teignm 4B **8**
Broadmeadow La.
TQ14: Bi'ton, Teignm 3A **8**
Broadmeadow Sports Cen. 4B **8**
Broadmeadow Vw.
TQ14: Teignm 3B **8**
Broad Oak Cres. TQ9: Tot 4G **31**
Broad Pk. TQ6: Dartm 4A **30**
Broadpark TQ13: Ashb 2F **33**
TQ13: Bov T 5A **4**
Broadpark Rd. TQ2: Torq 6F **19**
TQ3: Paig 3C **22**
Broadpath TQ9: Sto G . . . . .6A **24** (not continuous)
Broad Reach TQ4: Broads 6F **25**
Broadridge Cl. TQ12: New A . . .1C **10**
BROADSANDS 6E **25**
Broadsands Av. TQ4: Broads 6F **25**
Broadsands Bend
TQ4: Broads 5F **25**
Broadsands Ct. TQ4: Broads 6E **25**
Broadsands Pk. Rd.
TQ4: Broads 5F **25**
Broadsands Rd. TQ4: Broads . . .6E **25**
Broad Steps *TQ5: Brixh 2D 28*
(off Higher St.)
Broadstone
TQ6: Dartm 1A **30** (3C **30**)
Broadstone Pk. Rd.
TQ2: Torq 6G **19**
Broadway Av. TQ12: Kingst 3E **7**
Broadway Rd. TQ12: Kingst 3D **6**
Brockhurst Pk. TQ3: Marl 1A **22**
Brocks La. TQ12: Teigng 5G **5**
Brompton Gdns. TQ1: Torq 4F **21**
Bronescombe Av. TQ14: Bi'ton . . .5H **9**
Bronshill M. TQ1: Torq 3C **20**
Bronshill Rd. TQ1: Torq 3C **20**
Brook Cl. EX7: Holc 1G **9**
TQ13: Bov T 3B **4**
Brook Ct. TQ5: Brixh 3C **28**
Brookdale Cl. TQ5: Brixh 3C **28**
Brookdale Ct. TQ5: Brixh 3C **28**
Brookdale Pk. TQ5: Brixh 3C **28**
Brookdale Ter. EX7: Daw 4E **3**
BROOKEADOR 2G **15**
Brookedor TQ12: Kingsk 2G **15**
Brookedor Gdns.
TQ12: Kingsk 2G **15**
Brookfield Cl. TQ3: Pres 3F **23**
TQ12: Kingst 3F **7**
Brookfield Dr. TQ14: Teignm 2E **9**
Brookfield Orchard
TQ12: Kingst 4F **7**
Brook Haven Cl.
TQ12: Kingsk 2G **15**
Brook Ho. *EX7: Daw 4C 2*
(off Church St.)
Brooklands *EX7: Daw 4D 2*
(off Alexandra Rd.)
TQ9: Tot 4H **31**
Brooklands La. TQ2: Torq 5H **19**
Brook La. TQ14: Shal 6B **8**
Brook Orchard TQ12: Kingsk . . .2G **15**
Brook Rd. TQ12: Ipp 5B **14**
Brookside TQ7: Kingsb 4B **34**
Brookside Cl. TQ14: Teignm 4C **8**
Brook St. EX7: Daw 4D **2**
Brookvale Cl. TQ14: Shal 6B **8**
Brookvale Orchard TQ14: Shal . . .6B **8**
Brook Way TQ12: Kingst 1E **7**
Broomborough Ct. TQ9: Tot 4E **31**
Broombrough Dr. *TQ9: Tot 4E 31*
(off Plymouth Rd.)
Broom Cl. EX7: Daw 1F **3**
Broomhill Way TQ2: Torq 6D **16**
Broom Pk. TQ2: Torq 4E **17**
Brow Hill TQ12: Heat 4F **5**
Brownhills Rd. TQ12: New A 2F **11**
Brownings End TQ12: E Ogw . . .4E **11**
Brownings Wlk. TQ12: E Ogw . . .4E **11**
Browns Bri. Rd. TQ2: Torq 5C **16**
Brownscombe Cl. TQ3: Marl 1A **22**
Brown's Hill TQ6: Dartm 1A **30**
Brunel Av. TQ2: Torq 3G **17**
Brunel Cl. TQ14: Teignm 3E **9**
Brunel Ct. EX7: Daw 4E **3**
BRUNEL LODGE 4F **11**
Brunel M. *TQ2: Torq 5A 20*
(off Solsbro Rd.)
Brunel Rd. TQ4: Broads 6F **25**
TQ12: New A 2A **12**
Brunswick Pl. EX7: Daw 4D **2**
Brunswick Sq. *TQ1: Torq 3A 20*
(off Teignmouth Rd.)
Brunswick St. TQ14: Teignm 5E **9**
Brunswick Ter. TQ1: Torq 3A **20**
Brutus Cen. *TQ9: Tot 4F 31*
(off Station Rd.)
Buckeridge Av. TQ14: Teignm . . .3D **8**
Buckeridge Rd. TQ14: Teignm . . .2D **8**
BUCKFAST 2B **32**
Buckfast Abbey 2C **32**
Buckfast Butterflies &
Dartmoor Otter Sanctuary
. . . . .4D **32**
Buckfast Cl. TQ11: Buck 3C **32**
BUCKFASTLEIGH 4B **32**
Buckfastleigh Miniature Railway
. . . . .4D **32**
Buckfastleigh Station
South Devon Railway 4D **32**
Buckfastleigh Swimming Pool
. . . . .5B **32**
Buckfast Rd. TQ11: Buck 2C **32**
BUCKLAND 3C **12**
Buckland Brake TQ12: New A . . .3B **12**
Buckland Hgts. TQ12: New A . . .2C **12**
Buckland Rd. TQ12: New A 3B **12**
(Buckland Brake, not continuous)
TQ12: New A 2C **12**
(Haytor Dr.)
Buckland Vw. TQ12: New A 1A **12**
Buckley St. TQ8: Salc 2H **35**
Bucks Cl. TQ13: Bov T 3C **4**
Bucks La. *TQ13: Bov T 3C 4*
(off Fore St.)
Buckwell Cl. TQ7: Kingsb 2C **34**
Buckwell Rd. TQ7: Kingsb 2C **34**
Budleigh Cl. TQ1: Torq 3E **21**
Bullands Cl. TQ13: Bov T 2B **4**
Buller Rd. TQ12: New A 3A **12**
Bull Ring TQ13: Ashb 4F **33**
Bunting Cl. TQ12: E Ogw 4F **11**
TQ14: Teignm 3C **8**
Burch Gdns. EX7: Daw 1E **3**
Burdouns Way
TQ12: Kingst, New A 1F **7**
Burke Rd. TQ9: Tot 3G **31**
Burleigh Rd. TQ2: Torq 2F **19**
Burnham Ct. *TQ12: Kingst 4F 7*
(off Orchid Av.)
Burnley Cl. TQ12: New A 1C **10**
Burnley Rd. TQ12: New A 1C **10**
Burn River Ri. TQ2: Torq 1E **19**
Burnthouse Hill TQ12: N Whil . . .6F **15**
Burridge Av. TQ2: Torq 4G **19**
Burridge La. TQ2: Torq 4B **20**
Burridge Rd. TQ2: Torq 4G **19**
Bursledon Ct. *EX7: Daw 4F 3*
(off E. Cliff Rd.)
Burton Pl. TQ5: Brixh 3D **28**
Burton St. TQ5: Brixh 4D **28**
Burton Villa Cl. TQ5: Brixh 3D **28**
Burwood Pl. TQ14: Teignm 3F **9**
Bury Rd. TQ12: New A 1G **11**
Bushell Rd. TQ12: New A 1F **11**
Bushmead Av. TQ12: Kingsk . . .2H **15**
Butland Av. TQ3: Pres 2F **23**
Butland Rd. TQ12: Kingst 3E **7**
Buttercombe Cl. TQ12: E Ogw . . .5E **11**
Butterlake TQ3: Marl 5A **18**
Butt's La. TQ12: Coff 5F **13**
Bygones Mus.
Torquay 1D **20**
Byron Rd. TQ1: Torq 1B **20**
Byter Mill La. TQ9: Sto G 6B **24**

C

Cabbage Hill TQ13: Ashb 5E **33**
Cabourg Cl. TQ8: Salc 2G **35**
Cadewell Cres. TQ2: Torq 6C **16**
Cadewell La. TQ2: Torq 1F **19**
Cadewell Pk. Rd. TQ2: Torq 6B **16**
Cad La. *TQ13: Ashb 4F 33*
(off Stapledon La.)
Cadwell Rd. TQ3: Paig 4E **23**
Calvados Pk. TQ12: Kingst 4G **7**
Camborne Cres. TQ4: Good 5E **25**
Cambrian Cl. TQ4: Coll M 1A **24**

Commons La.—Downfield Cl.

Commons La. EX7: Daw 3D 2
TQ14: Shal 6B 8
Commons Old Rd.
TQ14: Shal 6C 8
(not continuous)
Compass Sth. TQ1: Torq 6G 21
COMPTON 3A 18
Compton Castle 3A 18
Compton Ho. TQ1: Torq 2D 20
(off Palermo Rd.)
Compton Pl. TQ1: Torq 6G 17
Condor Dr. TQ2: Torq 5C 16
Condor Way TQ2: Torq 5C 16
Congella Rd. TQ1: Torq 3D 20
Conifers, The TQ2: Torq 4G 17
TQ13: Bov T 6B 4
Coniston Cl. TQ5: Brixh 5B 28
Coniston Ct. TQ4: Paig 1D 24
Coniston Rd. TQ12: E Ogw 5E 11
Conniford La. TQ12: Ipp 6B 14
Connybear La. TQ12: Coff 6E 13
Conway Cres. TQ4: Paig 6D 22
Conway Rd. TQ4: Paig 6E 23
Cooke Dr. TQ12: Ipp 5C 14
Cooks Cl. TQ12: Kingst 4G 7
TQ13: Ashb 3G 33
Cookworthy Rd. TQ7: Kingsb 3B 34
COOMBE 2C 8
Coombe, The TQ5: Galm 2E 27
TQ6: Dartm 3C 30
Coombe Av. TQ14: Teignm 4C 8
Coombe Cl. TQ6: Dartm 3C 30
TQ13: Bov T 3D 4
Coombe Cross TQ13: Bov T 3D 4
Coombe La. TQ2: Torq 6F 17
TQ13: Bov T 3D 4
TQ14: Teignm 2C 8
Coombe Mdw. TQ13: Bov T 3D 4
Coombe Pk. Cotts. TQ1: Torq 6F 17
Coombe Pk. Rd.
TQ14: Teignm 3C 8
Coombe Rd. TQ3: Pres 2E 23
TQ6: Dartm 3C 30
TQ14: Shal 6A 8
Coombesend Rd.
TQ12: Kingst 4G 7
(not continuous)
Coombesend Rd. E.
TQ12: Kingst 4H 7
Coombeshead Rd.
TQ12: New A 1E 11
Coombe Shute TQ9: Sto G 6A 24
Coombe Va. Rd.
TQ14: Teignm 3C 8
Coombe Vw. TQ14: Teignm 2B 8
Coombe Way TQ14: Bi'ton 3A 8
Copland La. TQ9: Tot 3E 31
Copland Mdws. TQ9: Tot 3E 31
Copley Cl. TQ3: Paig 5C 22
Copperwood Cl. TQ13: Ashb 4E 33
Coppice, The EX7: Daw 6D 2
Copp Path EX7: Daw 5C 2
(off Taylor Cl.)
Copse, The TQ12: New A 3D 12
Copythorne Cl. TQ5: Brixh 3B 28
Copythorne Pk. TQ5: Brixh 3B 28
Copythorne Rd.
TQ5: Brixh, Chur F 2H 27
Corfe Cres. TQ2: Torq 1A 20
Cormorant Cl. TQ2: Torq 4C 16
Cornacre Cl. TQ2: Torq 2F 19
Cornacre Rd. TQ2: Torq 3F 19
Cornerstone TQ9: Tot 4F 31
(off Warland)
Cornfield Grn. TQ2: Torq 5G 17
(off Bellrock Cl.)
Corn Pk. Rd. TQ12: A'well 1B 14
Coronation Av. EX7: Daw 5D 2
Coronation Rd. TQ7: Kingsb 3C 34
TQ8: Salc 2G 35
TQ9: Tot 3F 31
TQ12: Kingst 4F 7
TQ12: New A 2F 11
Coronation St. TQ14: Shal 6C 8
Corsham Rd. TQ4: Paig 6D 22
Coryton Cl. EX7: Daw 4D 2
Cotehele Dr. TQ3: Paig 4A 22
Cotmore Cl. TQ5: Brixh 5B 28
Cotswold Cl. TQ2: Torq 6G 19
Cottey Mdw. TQ12: Kingst 5F 7
County Court
Torquay & Newton Abbot
....6D 16
Courtenay Gdns.
TQ12: New A 3H 11
Courtenay Mnr. TQ1: Torq 5D 20
(off Grafton Rd.)
Courtenay Pk. TQ12: New A 2A 12
Courtenay Pl. TQ14: Teignm 5E 9
(off Den Promenade)
Courtenay Rd. TQ4: Good 3F 25
TQ12: New A 3G 11
Courtenay St. TQ8: Salc 2G 35
TQ12: New A 2G 11
Courtenay Ter. TQ8: Salc 2G 35
(off Devon Rd.)
Court Farm Barn
TQ12: A'well 1C 14
Courtfield TQ9: Tot 4H 31
Court Ga. Cl. TQ12: Ipp 6A 14
Court Grange TQ12: A'well 1B 14
Court Grange La.
TQ12: A'well 1A 14
Courtlage Wlk. TQ7: Kingsb 2B 34
Courtland Rd. TQ2: Torq 2E 19
TQ3: Paig 4E 23
Courtlands Rd. TQ12: New A 3A 12
Court M. TQ12: New A 2G 11
(off Wolborough St.)
Court Rd. TQ2: Torq 4F 19
TQ12: A'well 1C 14
Courtyard, The TQ12: New A 2G 11
(off Wolborough St.)
Cousens Cl. EX7: Daw 2F 3
Coventry Farm Trad. Est.
TQ12: Kingsk 5H 15
Coverdale Ct. TQ3: Paig 5E 23
(off Bishops Pl.)
Coverdale Rd. TQ3: Paig 5E 23
Coxs Steps TQ6: Dartm 1A 30
(off Clarence Hill)
Crabshell Hgts. TQ7: Kingsb 5C 34
Cranford Rd. TQ3: Pres 2D 22
Creek Rd. TQ6: Dartm 3A 30
Crescent, The TQ5: Brixh 4E 29
Crescent Ct. TQ6: Dartm 4A 30
(off Townstal Cres.)
Cresswell Cl. TQ12: Kingsk 2H 15
Crestas, The TQ1: Torq 3D 20
Crest Hill TQ11: B'leigh 4B 32
Crest Vw. TQ4: Paig 6F 23
Cricketers Grn. TQ2: Torq 1H 19
Cricket Fld. Rd.
TQ12: New A 1H 11
Cricketfield Rd. TQ2: Torq 2H 19
Cricket La. TQ11: B'leigh 3A 32
Crispin Rd. TQ7: Kingsb 3B 34
Croft, The TQ12: E Ogw 4C 10
Croft Cl. TQ12: E Ogw 4C 10
Croft Ct. TQ2: Torq 4B 20
(off Abbey Rd.)
Croft Hill TQ2: Torq 4B 20
Croft Mdw. TQ12: Ipp 5B 14
Croft Orchard TQ12: Ipp 5B 14
Croft Rd. TQ2: Torq 4B 20
TQ8: Salc 2G 35
TQ12: E Ogw 4B 10
TQ12: Ipp 5B 14
Croftview Ter. TQ8: Salc 2G 35
(off Island St.)
Croker's Mdw. TQ13: Bov T 2B 4
Crokers Way TQ12: Ipp 5B 14
Cromartie Point TQ2: Torq 1H 23
(off Livermead Hill)
Cromwells Way TQ13: Bov T 2B 4
Croppins Cl. TQ11: B'leigh 4C 32
Cross Grange Trad. Est.
TQ12: Heat 3E 5
Cross Hill TQ12: C'head, Neth 2F 13
Cross La. TQ8: E Port 3H 35
TQ12: Neth 1G 13
Crossley Cl. TQ12: Kingst 3F 7
Crossley Moor Rd.
TQ12: Kingst 4F 7
Cross Pk. TQ5: Brixh 4C 28
TQ12: Neth 1G 13
Crosspark TQ9: Tot 3H 31
Crosspark Av. TQ2: Torq 1F 19
Crossparks TQ6: Dartm 5A 30
Crossway TQ4: Good 3F 25
Crossways Shop. Cen., The
TQ4: Paig 5E 23
Crown & Anchor Way
TQ3: Paig 5E 23
Crownhill Ct. TQ2: Torq 3H 19
Crownhill Cres. TQ5: Galm 2E 27
Crownhill Pk. TQ2: Torq 3H 19
Crownhill Ri. TQ2: Torq 3H 19
Crownley La. TQ9: Sto G 5A 24
Crown Sq. TQ14: Shal 6C 8
Crowther's Hill
TQ6: Dartm 2A 30 (4C 30)
Crystal Cl. TQ4: Good 3F 25
Cudhill Rd. TQ5: Brixh 3C 28
Culm Cl. TQ2: Torq 1E 19
Culverdale TQ9: Tot 5H 31
Culver Pk. Cl. TQ7: Kingsb 5D 34
Culvery Grn. TQ2: Torq 1E 19
Cumber Cl. TQ5: Brixh 2C 28
Cumber Dr. TQ5: Brixh 2C 28
Cumberland Grn. TQ5: Brixh 2C 28
Curledge St. TQ4: Paig 6E 23
Curlew Cl. TQ2: Torq 4B 16
Custom Ho. Hill TQ14: Teignm 5D 8
Cuthbert Cl. TQ1: Torq 6F 17
Cypress Cl. TQ2: Torq 4B 20
Cypress Ct. TQ4: Paig 6E 23
(off Fisher St.)

D

Daccabridge Rd.
TQ12: Kingsk 3G 15
DACCOMBE 3D 16
Daccombe Hill TQ12: Dacc 3D 16
Daccombe Mill La.
TQ12: Coff, Kingsk 3H 15
Daddyhole Plain TQ1: Torq 6E 21
Daddyhole Rd. TQ1: Torq 6D 20
(not continuous)
Daggers Copse TQ12: New A 2E 11
Dagmar St. TQ14: Shal 6C 8
Dagra La. TQ14: Shal 6A 8
Daimonds La. TQ14: Teignm 4D 8
Dainton Ct. TQ4: Good 3F 25
Dainton M. TQ4: Paig 6E 23
Dainton Pk. Golf Course 4A 14
Dairy Hill TQ2: Torq 2F 19
Daison Cotts. TQ1: Torq 2B 20
Daison Cres. TQ1: Torq 1C 20
Dalverton Ct. TQ5: Brixh 1D 28
Danby Hgts. Cl. TQ1: Torq 5F 21
Dane Heath Bus. Pk.
TQ12: Heat 3E 5
Danvers Rd. TQ2: Torq 5E 17
Daphne Cl. TQ1: Torq 5E 21
D'arcy Ct. TQ12: New A 1H 11
Darky La. TQ7: Kingsb 1A 34
Darran Cl. TQ12: Kingst 4G 7
Darran Rd. TQ12: Kingst 4G 7
Dart Av. TQ2: Torq 1F 19
Dartbridge Mnr. TQ11: B'leigh 3C 32
Dart Bri. Rd. TQ11: B'leigh 4C 32
Dartington La. TQ9: Darti 2E 31
Dart Marina TQ6: Dartm 2C 30
Dartmoor Ct. TQ13: Bov T 3B 4
(off Station Rd.)
Dartmoor National Pk.
....6A 4, 3A 32 & 1E 33
DARTMOUTH 1B 30 (4C 30)
DARTMOUTH & KINGSWEAR
HOSPITAL 2B 30 (4C 30)
Dartmouth Ct. TQ6: Dartm 2B 30
(off Oxford St.)
Dartmouth Mus. 1B 30 (4C 30)
Dartmouth Outdoor Heated Pool
....5A 30
Dartmouth Rd.
TQ4: Broads, Good, Paig 5E 23
TQ5: Chur F 1E 27
Dartmouth Steam Railway
Churston Station 2F 27
Goodrington Station 1F 25
Kingswear Station 4D 30
Paignton Station 6E 23
Dartmouth Yacht Club 2B 30
Darton Gro. TQ9: Sto G 6A 24
Dart Rock 4D 32
Dartside TQ9: Tot 2E 31
Dartside Ct. TQ6: Dartm 3C 30
(off Clarence St.)
Dartside Quay TQ5: Galm 3D 26
Dart Vw. Rd. TQ5: Galm 1E 27
Dart Vs. TQ9: Tot 5F 31
Darwin Ct. TQ2: Torq 4E 17
Darwin Cres. TQ2: Torq 4E 17
Dashpers TQ5: Brixh 4C 28
David Rd. TQ3: Paig 4D 22
Davies Av. TQ4: Good 4E 25
Davis Av. TQ2: Torq 3G 19
Davis Ct. TQ12: New A 1F 11
Davis Rd. TQ6: Dartm 4A 30
Dawes Cl. TQ12: E Ogw 5E 11
DAWLISH 4E 3
Dawlish Bus. Pk. EX7: Daw 1F 3
DAWLISH COMMUNITY HOSPITAL
....4D 2
Dawlish Leisure Cen. 2F 3
Dawlish Mus. 4D 2
Dawlish Rd. TQ14: Teignm 4E 9
Dawlish Station (Rail) 4E 3
Dawlish St. TQ14: Teignm 4E 9
DAWLISH WARREN 1G 3
Dawlish Warren Rd.
EX7: Daw W 1H 3
Dawlish Warren Station (Rail) 1H 3
Daws Mdw. TQ12: Kingst 5F 7
Deans Cl. TQ14: Bi'ton 5G 9
De Courcy Rd. TQ8: Salc 5E 35
Decoy Country Pk. 4H 11
Decoy Discovery Cen. 4A 12
Decoy Ind. Est. TQ12: New A 5A 12
Decoy Rd. TQ12: New A 3A 12
Deep Dene Cl. TQ5: Brixh 4B 28
Deer Pk. Av. TQ14: Teignm 3C 8
Deer Pk. Cl. TQ14: Teignm 3C 8
Deer Pk. Dr. TQ14: Teignm 3C 8
Deerpark La. TQ12: Hacc 6G 13
Deer Pk. Rd. TQ12: New A 4A 12
Deers Leap Cl. TQ3: Pres 1E 23
Den, The TQ14: Teignm 5E 9
Den Brook Cl. TQ1: Torq 3E 21
DENBURY 6A 10
Denbury Rd.
TQ12: Den, E Ogw 6C 10
Denby Ho. TQ4: Paig 6F 23
Den Cres. TQ14: Teignm 5E 9
Dendy Rd. TQ4: Paig 5E 23
Den Prom. TQ14: Teignm 5E 9
Den Rd. TQ14: Teignm 5E 9
Denys Rd. TQ1: Torq 3D 20
TQ9: Tot 4F 31
Derby Rd. TQ7: Kingsb 4C 34
Derncleugh Gdns. EX7: Holc 1H 9
Derrell Rd. TQ4: Paig 1D 24
Derwent Rd. TQ1: Torq 2C 20
De Tracey Pk. TQ13: Bov T 3C 4
Devon Bird of Prey Centre, The
....3A 14
Devoncourt TQ5: Brixh 1F 29
Devondale Ct. EX7: Daw W 1H 3
Devon Heath TQ13: Chud K 1H 5
Devon Ho. Dr. TQ13: Bov T 2D 4
Devon Ho. Flats TQ13: Bov T 2D 4
Devon M. TQ13: Chud K 1H 5
(off Devon Heath)
Devon Pl. TQ9: Tot 4G 31
(off Bridgetown)
Devon Rd. TQ8: Salc 4F 35
Devonshire Ho. TQ1: Torq 1D 20
Devon Sq. TQ7: Kingsb 3B 34
TQ12: New A 2H 11
Devons Rd. TQ1: Torq 2D 20
Devon Ter. TQ9: Tot 4G 31
Devon Valley Holiday Village
TQ14: Shal 6A 8
Devon Vw. EX7: Daw W 1H 3
Devon Windsurf & Canoe Cen.
....4H 11
Dickers Ter. TQ12: Kingst 4F 7
Diptford Cl. TQ4: Paig 2B 24
DITTISHAM 4A 26
Dittisham Sailing Club 4A 26
Dixon Cl. TQ3: Paig 2B 22
Dobbin Arch TQ12: Kingsk 3G 15
Doctors Rd. TQ5: Brixh 4D 28
DODBROOKE 3D 34
Dodbrooke Ct. TQ7: Kingsb 3C 34
Dolbeare Rd. TQ13: Ashb 3G 33
(not continuous)
Dolphin Ct. TQ5: Brixh 2D 28
TQ14: Shal 6C 8
(off Albion St.)
Dolphin Ct. Rd. TQ3: Pres 2C 22
Dolphin Cres. TQ3: Pres 2C 22
Dorchester Gro. TQ2: Torq 6E 17
Dornafield Cl. TQ12: Ipp 5B 14
Dornafield Dr. E. TQ12: Ipp 5B 14
Dornafield Dr. W. TQ12: Ipp 5B 14
Dornafield Rd. TQ12: Ipp 5B 14
Dosson Gro. TQ1: Torq 2H 19
Doughy La. TQ12: Den 6A 10
Douglas Av. TQ5: Brixh 3F 29
Douglas Ho. TQ14: Teignm 4D 8
(off Bitton Pk. Rd.)
Dower Ct. TQ3: Pres 3F 23
Dower Rd. TQ1: Torq 2B 20
Downaway La. TQ12: Dacc 1D 16
Downfield Cl. TQ5: Brixh 4B 28

Dragoon Cl.—Furzeham Pk.

Dragoon Cl. TQ12: Heat 6D 4
Drake Av. TQ2: Torq 3F 19
TQ14: Teignm 1C 8
Drake Dr. TQ4: Good 3D 24
Drake La. TQ13: Bov T 3D 4
Drake Rd. TQ8: Salc 2F 35
TQ12: New A 2C 12
TQ13: Bov T 3D 4
Drakes Rd. TQ4: Paig 1B 24
Drew's Fld. La.
TQ3: Comp 2A 18
Drew St. TQ5: Brixh 4D 28
Drive, The EX7: Daw 4E 3
TQ5: Brixh 5D 28
TQ14: Bi'ton 5F 9
Druid Rd. TQ13: Ashb 1E 33
Drum Way TQ12: Heat 4E 5
Duchy Av. TQ3: Pres 1D 22
Duchy Dr. TQ3: Pres 1D 22
Duchy Gdns. TQ3: Pres 6D 18
Duchy Pk. TQ3: Pres 1D 22
Duckspond Cl. TQ11: B'leigh . . .5A 32
Duckspond Rd. TQ11: B'leigh . . .5A 32
Dukes Cl. TQ3: Paig 5B 22
Dukes Rd. TQ9: Tot 4H 31
Duke St. TQ6: Dartm . . .1A 30 (4C 30)
TQ7: Kingsb 3B 34
Dulverton M. TQ3: Paig 3B 22
Dunboyne Ct. *TQ1: Torq 1C 20*
(off St Marychurch Rd.)
Duncannon La. TQ9: Sto G 6A 24
Duncannon Mead TQ9: Sto G . . .6A 24
Duncombe St. TQ7: Kingsb 2C 34
Dunmere Rd. TQ1: Torq 3C 20
Dunmore Ct. TQ14: Shal 6D 8
Dunmore Dr. TQ14: Shal 6D 8
Dunning Rd. TQ14: Teignm 2C 8
Dunning Wlk. *TQ14: Teignm 2C 8*
(off Lake Av.)
Dunstone Cl. TQ3: Paig 2B 22
Dunstone Pk. Rd. TQ3: Paig 2B 22
Dunstone Ri. TQ3: Paig 2B 22
Durham Cl. TQ3: Pres 2E 23
Durleigh Rd. TQ5: Brixh 3C 28

E

Eagle Cl. TQ12: Kingst 1E 7
Eaglewood Cl. TQ2: Torq 5B 16
Ealing Cl. TQ5: Brixh 4E 29
Earls Ct. TQ1: Torq 3A 20
Earlswood Dr. TQ3: Paig 4A 22
E. Cliff Cl. EX7: Daw 3E 3
Eastcliffe Ho. TQ14: Teignm 3F 9
E. Cliff Gdns. EX7: Daw 3E 3
E. Cliff Rd. EX7: Daw 3E 3
Eastcliff Wlk. TQ14: Teignm 4F 9
East End Ter. TQ13: Ashb 2H 33
Easterfield La. TQ1: Torq 5G 17
Eastern Backway
TQ7: Kingsb 3C 34
(off Church St.)
Eastern Esplanade TQ3: Paig . . .6F 23
TQ4: Paig 6F 23
Eastern Rd. TQ13: Ashb 3G 33
EAST OGWELL 4C 10
E. Pafford Av. TQ2: Torq 5G 17
EAST PORTLEMOUTH 3H 35
East St. TQ2: Torq 3A 20
TQ12: Den 6A 10
TQ12: Ipp 5B 14
TQ12: New A 2G 11
TQ13: Ashb 4F 33
TQ13: Bov T 2C 4
Eastwood Cres. TQ12: New A . . .1D 10
Eaton Ct. TQ14: Teignm 2D 8
Eaton Hill Dr. *TQ6: Dartm 3B 30*
(off Flagstaff Rd.)
Eaton Pl. TQ4: Paig 6E 23
Ebdon Way TQ1: Torq 3A 20
Ebenezer Rd. TQ3: Paig 6D 22
Ebrington St. TQ7: Kingsb 3C 34
Eden Cl. TQ5: Brixh 4D 28
Eden Gro. TQ3: Paig 4C 22
Edenhurst Ct. *TQ1: Torq 6C 20*
(off Parkhill Rd.)
Eden Pk. TQ5: Brixh 4D 28
Edens Ct. *TQ14: Teignm 4E 9*
(off Heywoods Rd.)
Eden Va. Rd. TQ3: Paig 3C 22
Edgelands La. TQ12: Ipp 6A 14
Edgeley Rd. TQ2: Torq 5F 17
EDGINSWELL 1F 19
Edginswell Cl. TQ2: Torq 6B 16
Edginswell La. TQ2: Torq 4G 15
TQ12: Kingsk 4G 15
Edinburgh Rd. TQ5: Brixh 4E 29
Edinburgh Vs. TQ1: Torq 3A 20
Edmonds Wlk. TQ1: Torq 3A 20
Egerton Rd. TQ1: Torq 3D 20
Elba Cl. TQ4: Good 4F 25
Elberry La. TQ4: Broads 6G 25
TQ5: Chur F 3G 27
Elizabeth Av. TQ5: Brixh 6B 28
Elizabeth Ct. TQ2: Torq 4A 20
Elizabeth Sq. TQ12: New A 3C 12
Elkins Hill TQ5: Brixh 2E 29
ELLACOMBE 3C 20
Ellacombe Chu. Rd.
TQ1: Torq 3C 20
Ellacombe Rd. TQ1: Torq 3C 20
Ellerslie Ho. *TQ14: Shal 6D 8*
(off Marine Pde.)
Ellesmere TQ1: Torq 5D 20
Ellesmere Rd. TQ1: Torq 4F 21
Elliott Ct. TQ12: Ipp 5B 14
Elliott Gro. TQ5: Brixh 3B 28
Elliott Plain TQ11: B'leigh 4C 32
Elm Bank TQ11: B'leigh 5A 32
Elmbank Gdns. TQ4: Paig 6D 22
Elmbank Rd. TQ4: Paig 6D 22
Elm Dr. TQ12: Kingst 4F 7
Elm Gro. TQ14: Teignm 1D 8
Elm Gro. Cl. EX7: Daw 3E 3
Elm Gro. Dr. EX7: Daw 3E 3
Elm Gro. Rd. EX7: Daw 2E 3
Elmhirst Dr. TQ9: Tot 4H 31
Elmhurst Ct. TQ14: Teignm 4D 8
El Monte Cl. TQ14: Teignm 3D 8
Elm Pk. TQ3: Paig 5C 22
Elm Rd. TQ5: Brixh 5B 28
TQ12: New A 2H 11
Elmsleigh Ct. *TQ4: Paig 6E 23*
(off Elmsleigh Rd.)
Elmsleigh Pk. TQ4: Paig 6E 23
Elmsleigh Rd. TQ4: Paig 6E 23
Elm Wlk. TQ9: Tot 4H 31
Elmwood Av. TQ12: New A 1D 10
Elmwood Cres. EX7: Daw 3E 3
Elsdale Rd. TQ4: Paig 1D 24
Embankment, The TQ14: Shal . . .6B 8
Embankment Rd.
TQ7: Kingsb 4C 34
Ember Rd. TQ8: Salc 2F 35
Emblett Dr. TQ12: New A 1D 10
Emblett Hill Vw.
TQ12: E Ogw 4E 11
Embury Cl. TQ12: Kingsk 3H 15
Emlyn Pl. TQ13: Bov T 3C 4
Emmetts Pk. TQ13: Ashb 3G 33
Emmetts Pl. TQ12: A'well 1C 14
Empire Ct. TQ1: Torq 2B 20
Empire Rd. TQ1: Torq 2B 20
Empsons Cl. EX7: Daw 4C 2
Empsons Hill EX7: Daw 4C 2
Enfield Rd. TQ1: Torq 2D 20
Erica Dr. TQ2: Torq 4E 17
Esplanade TQ14: Teignm 5E 9
Esplanade, The TQ4: Paig 6F 23
TQ6: Dartm 2C 30
Esplanade Rd. TQ3: Paig 6F 23
TQ4: Paig 6F 23
Eugene Rd. TQ3: Pres 3F 23
Eureka Ter. TQ13: Bov T 2C 4
Eveleigh Cl. TQ5: Brixh 4D 28
Exe Hill TQ2: Torq 1E 19
Exeter Av. TQ2: Torq 6E 17
Exeter Rd. EX7: Daw 1F 3
TQ12: Kingst 1E 7
TQ12: Kingst, New A 5C 6
TQ12: New A 6A 6
TQ14: Teignm 2C 8
Exeter St. TQ14: Teignm 4D 8
Explorer Wlk. *TQ2: Torq 4E 17*
(off Kingsley Av.)

F

Factory Row TQ2: Torq 4B 20
Fairfax Pl.
TQ6: Dartm 2B 30 (4C 30)
Fairfax Rd. TQ12: Heat . . .6D 4 & 3E 5
Fairfield Cl. TQ7: Kingsb 4C 34
TQ13: Bov T 3B 4
Fairfield Rd. TQ2: Torq 1A 20
TQ12: Kingsk 4H 15
Fairfield Ter. TQ12: New A 2H 11
Fairies Hill TQ11: B'leigh 3C 32
Fair Isle Cl. TQ2: Torq 5D 16
Fairlawns Pk. TQ4: Good 3E 25
Fairlea Cl. EX7: Daw 1F 3
Fairlea Rd. EX7: Daw 2E 3
Fair Oaks TQ14: Teignm 3C 8
Fairseat Cl. TQ9: Tot 4G 31
Fairview Rd.
TQ6: Dartm 1A 30 (4B 30)
TQ12: Den 6A 10
Fairwater Cl. TQ12: Kingst 4G 7
Fairwaters TQ12: Kingst 3F 7
Fairway Cl. TQ5: Chur F 2G 27
Fairy La. TQ11: B'leigh 5A 32
Falkland Dr. TQ12: Kingst 3G 7
Falkland Rd. TQ2: Torq 5A 20
Falkland Way TQ14: Teignm 2C 8
Fallowfields *TQ9: Tot 4E 31*
(off Plymouth Rd.)
Falloway Cl. TQ2: Torq 5F 17
Fallowfield Cl. TQ12: New A . . .2C 12
Falmouth Cl. TQ2: Torq 1E 19
Farm Cl. TQ12: Kingsk 1G 15
Farmyard La. TQ3: Comp 3A 18
Farthing La. TQ3: Marl 1A 22
Farwell Rd. TQ9: Tot 4E 31
Faulkner Cl. TQ6: Dartm 4A 30
Fay Rd. EX7: Daw 4E 3
Fern Cl. TQ5: Brixh 3E 29
Ferncombe Cl. TQ12: Kingst 1F 7
Ferncombe Dr. TQ12: Kingst 1F 7
Ferndale TQ6: Dartm . . .2A 30 (4B 30)
Ferndale M. TQ2: Torq 2E 19
Ferndale Rd. TQ2: Torq 2E 19
TQ14: Teignm 3D 8
Fernham Ter. TQ3: Paig 4E 23
Fernicombe Cl. TQ3: Paig 4B 22
Fernicombe Rd. TQ3: Paig 4B 22
Fern Rd. TQ12: New A 5C 12
Fernworthy Cl. TQ2: Torq 2D 18
Ferrers Grn. TQ5: Chur F 3H 27
Ferrymans Reach *TQ14: Shal 6D 8*
(off Marine Pde.)
Field Cl. TQ3: Pres 1E 23
Firbank Rd. EX7: Daw 1F 3
Firestone La. TQ12: A'well 6F 11
Firlands TQ14: Teignm 2D 8
Firlands Rd. TQ2: Torq 5F 17
Firleigh Rd. TQ12: Kingst 2E 7
First Av. EX7: Daw 5C 2
TQ1: Torq 1B 20
TQ14: Teignm 4C 8
First Dr. TQ14: Teignm 4D 8
(Second Dr.)
TQ14: Teignm 3F 9
(The Rowdens)
Fir Wlk. TQ2: Torq 1F 19
Fishacre Cl. TQ3: Paig 3B 22
Fishchowter's La. TQ9: Tot 5F 31
Fishcombe Rd. TQ5: Brixh 1C 28
Fisher Rd. TQ12: New A 2G 11
Fisher St. TQ4: Paig 6E 23
Five Acres TQ13: Bov T 6B 4
Five Lanes Rd. TQ3: Marl 1A 22
Flagstaff Rd. TQ6: Dartm 3B 30
Flats, The EX7: Daw 1E 3
Flavel Arts Centre, The 1A 30
(off Flavel Pl.)
Flavel Pl. TQ6: Dartm 1A 30
Flavel St. TQ6: Dartm 1A 30
Fleet Ct. TQ1: Torq 5C 20
Fleet St. TQ1: Torq 5C 20
TQ2: Torq 5C 20
Fleet Wlk. *TQ2: Torq 5C 20*
(off Fleet St.)
Fleet Wlk. Shop. Cen.
TQ2: Torq 5C 20
Flemons Ct. *TQ4: Paig 6D 22*
(off St Michael's Rd.)
Fletcher Cl. TQ2: Torq 2H 19
Flete Av. TQ12: New A 3C 12
Flete Cl. TQ12: New A 3C 12
Flood St. TQ9: Sto G 5A 24
Florence Pl. TQ12: New A 3A 12
Florida Rd. TQ1: Torq 4D 20
Flow La. TQ14: Bi'ton 6G 9
(not continuous)
Fluder Cres. TQ12: Kingsk 4A 16
Fluder Hill TQ12: Kingsk 3H 15
Fluder La. TQ12: Dacc 2E 17
Fluder Ri. TQ12: Kingsk 4A 16
Foales Ct. *TQ13: Ashb 4F 33*
(off North St.)
Follafield Pk. TQ5: Brixh 5C 28
Folly La. *TQ8: Salc 2H 35*
(off Fore St.)
Fonthill TQ1: Torq 5E 21
Football La. TQ12: Kingst 3F 7
Footland La. TQ12: Dacc 2D 16
Footlands Rd. TQ4: Paig 1D 24
Forbes Cl. TQ12: Heat 4E 5
FORCHES CROSS 4A 6
Ford TQ6: Dartm 4B 30
Forde Cl. TQ12: A'well 6F 11
TQ12: New A 2A 12
Fordens La. EX7: Holc 1G 9
Forde Pk. TQ12: New A 3A 12
Forde Pl. TQ12: New A 3A 12
Forder La. TQ14: Bi'ton 5F 9
(not continuous)
Forde Rd. TQ12: New A 2A 12
Forde Vs. TQ12: New A 3A 12
Ford Pk. TQ13: Chud K 1H 5
Ford Rd. TQ9: Tot 3G 31
TQ12: A'well 6G 11
Ford Valley TQ6: Dartm 4B 30
Foredown La. TQ12: Kingsk 3F 15
Foresters Ter. TQ14: Teignm 5D 8
Fore St. TQ1: Torq 1C 20
TQ2: Torq 4E 17
TQ5: Brixh 2D 28
TQ6: Kingsw 4D 30
TQ7: Kingsb 3B 34
TQ8: Salc 2H 35
TQ9: Tot 4F 31
TQ11: B'leigh 4B 32
TQ12: Ipp 5B 14
TQ12: Kingsk 3G 15
TQ12: Kingst 4F 7
TQ13: Bov T 3C 4
TQ14: Bi'ton 5G 9
TQ14: Shal 6C 8
TQ14: Teignm 4D 8
(not continuous)
Forest Ridge Rd. TQ3: Pres 2C 22
Forest Rd. TQ1: Torq 3B 20
Forge Pl. TQ13: Bov T 3B 4
Forgeway Cl. TQ2: Torq 5G 19
Forster Rd. TQ8: Salc 2G 35
Fortescue Rd. TQ3: Pres 2F 23
TQ8: Salc 3F 35
Fortune Way TQ1: Torq 2C 20
Fosse Rd. TQ7: Kingsb 2C 34
Foss Slip TQ6: Dartm 1A 30
Foss St. TQ6: Dartm . . .1A 30 (4C 30)
Fountain Ct. *TQ13: Bov T 3C 4*
(off Fore St.)
TQ14: Teignm 5E 9
(off Triangle Pl.)
Fouracre Way TQ12: Kingst 3G 7
Fourcross Units TQ9: Sto G 5B 24
Fourth Av. TQ14: Teignm 3C 8
Fourview Cl. TQ5: Brixh 3F 29
Fowey Av. TQ2: Torq 1E 19
Foxhole Rd. TQ2: Torq 5G 19
TQ3: Paig 5C 22
Foxhollows TQ12: New A 3D 12
Foxlands TQ1: Torq 2D 20
Foxlands Wlk. *TQ1: Torq 1D 20*
(off Fore St.)
Foxley Cres. TQ12: New A 2E 11
Fox Tor Cl. TQ4: Good 6E 25
Foxwell La. TQ12: New A 1F 11
Franeth Cl. TQ12: Kingst 3E 7
Fraser Ct. TQ3: Paig 6C 22
Fraser Dr. TQ14: Teignm 3C 8
Frederick Ter. *EX7: Daw 4D 2*
(off Stockton Rd.)
Freestone Rd. TQ12: Kingst 3E 7
French St. TQ14: Teignm 4E 9
Freshwater Dr. TQ4: Good 5D 24
Frobisher Cl. TQ14: Teignm 1C 8
Frobisher Grn. TQ2: Torq 3F 19
Frobisher La. TQ8: Salc 2F 35
Frobisher Rd. TQ12: New A 1C 12
Frobisher Way TQ4: Good 3E 25
Frogmore Ter. TQ7: Kingsb 4B 34
Froude Av. TQ2: Torq 3G 17
Froude Rd. TQ8: Salc 5E 35
Fullaford Pk. TQ11: B'leigh 5A 32
Fulton Cl. TQ12: Ipp 5B 14
Furlong Cl. TQ11: Buck 2B 32
Furness Cl. TQ4: Paig 3D 24
Furrough Ct. TQ1: Torq 1D 20
Furrough Cross TQ1: Torq 1D 20
Furze Cap TQ12: Kingst 1E 7
Furzedown Rd. TQ12: Kingsk . . .2H 15
Furze Gdns. TQ9: Tot 4H 31
Furzegood TQ3: Marl 1A 22
Furzeham Ct. TQ5: Brixh 2C 28
Furzeham Pk. TQ5: Brixh 2D 28

Furzehill Rd. TQ1: Torq 3B **20**
Furze La. TQ5: Brixh 2E **29**
Furzeleigh La. TQ13: Bov T 2B **4**
Furze Rd. TQ9: Tot 4H **31**

G

Gabwell La. TQ12: S'head 1G **17**
Gainsborough Cl. TQ1: Torq 5E **21**
Gala Bingo
Torquay 4B **20**
Gales Crest TQ13: Chud K 1H **5**
Gallants Bower Fort 6D **30**
Gallery, The *TQ2: Torq . . . . .5C 20* *(off Fleet St.)*
Galloway Dr. TQ14: Teignm 2B **8**
GALMPTON 2E **27**
Galmpton Ct. *TQ5: Galm . . . . . . .2E 27* *(off Galmpton Farm Cl.)*
Galmpton Farm Cl. TQ5: Galm 2E **27**
Galmpton Glade TQ5: Galm 2E **27**
Galmpton Touring Pk. TQ5: Galm 3E **27**
GALMPTON WARBOROUGH . . .6E **25**
Ganders Pk. TQ2: Torq 6H **15**
Gard Cl. TQ2: Torq 4F **17**
Garden Mill Ind. Est. TQ7: Kingsb 4C **34**
Garden Rd. TQ1: Torq 3C **20**
Garfield Rd. TQ4: Paig 5F **23**
Garlic Rea TQ5: Brixh . . . . .2E **29** (not continuous)
Garners Cl. TQ12: E Ogw 4C **10**
Garners La. TQ12: E Ogw 4C **10**
Garrow Cl. TQ5: Brixh 4D **28**
Garston Av. TQ12: New A 1G **11**
Garth Rd. TQ2: Torq 5F **17**
Gatehouse Barns EX7: Daw 2E **3**
Gatehouse Cl. EX7: Daw 3D **2**
Gatehouse Hill EX7: Daw 3E **3**
Gatehouse Ri. EX7: Daw 3E **3**
Gate Tree Cl. TQ12: Kingst 4G **7**
Gattery La. TQ5: Brixh 6A **28**
Gaze Hill TQ12: New A 6A **6**
Gentian Cl. TQ3: Marl 1A **22**
George Rd. TQ3: Pres 2E **23**
George St. TQ12: New A 2G **11**
TQ14: Teignm 5E **9**
Georgian Ct. TQ1: Torq 3F **21**
Gerston La. TQ7: Kingsb 6B **34**
Gerston Pl. TQ3: Paig 5E **23**
Gerston Rd. TQ4: Paig 5E **23**
Gerstons, The TQ3: Paig 5E **23**
Gestridge Rd. TQ12: Kingst 3E **7**
Gibson Ct. TQ4: Good 4D **24**
Gibson Dr. TQ4: Good 4D **24**
Gibson Gdns. TQ4: Good 4D **24**
Gibson Rd. TQ4: Good 4D **24**
Gilbert Av. TQ14: Teignm 2C **8**
Gilbert Cl. TQ2: Torq 3G **19**
Gilbert Rd. TQ12: New A 2B **12**
Gilbert Way TQ4: Good 3D **24**
Gillard Rd. TQ5: Brixh 3F **29**
Gills Nursery *TQ9: Tot . . . . .4F 31* *(off South St.)*
Gilpin Cl. EX7: Daw 2F **3**
Gipsy La. TQ11: B'leigh 6A **32**
Gladstone Pl. TQ12: New A 2H **11**
Gladstone Ter. TQ14: Teignm 4E **9**
Glebe, The TQ12: Ipp 5A **14**
Glebe Cl. TQ12: New A 2E **11**
Glebelands TQ11: B'leigh 3A **32**
Glebeland Way TQ2: Torq 1E **19**
Glen, The TQ12: New A 3C **12**
Glenarm Ter. *TQ9: Tot . . . . .3F 31* *(off Castle St.)*
Glencarnock Cl. TQ1: Torq 2H **19**
Glendale Ter. *TQ9: Tot . . . . .3F 31* *(off Castle St.)*
Glendaragh Rd. TQ14: Teignm . . .4E **9**
Glenmore Rd. TQ5: Brixh 3D **28**
Glen Rd. TQ3: Paig 4E **23**
Glenside Cl. TQ14: Teignm 3D **8**
Glenthorne Cl. TQ1: Torq 5E **21**
Gloucester Cl. TQ2: Torq 6E **17**
Gloucester Rd.
TQ12: New A 3H **11**
TQ14: Teignm 4D **8**
Godfrey Av. TQ3: Pres 1E **23**
Golden Cl. TQ5: Brixh 5C **28**
Golden Hind 2E **29**
Golden Lion Ct. TQ13: Ashb 4F **33**
Golden Pk. Av. TQ2: Torq 4E **17**
Golden Sands Holiday Pk. EX7: Daw W 1G **3**
Golden Ter. EX7: Daw 4D **2**
Gollands TQ5: Brixh 2C **28**
Gollands Cl. TQ5: Brixh 2B **28**
Golvers Hill Cl. TQ12: Kingst 4F **7**
Golvers Hill Rd. TQ12: Kingst 4F **7**
Goodridge Cl. EX7: Daw 2E **3**
GOODRINGTON 4D **24**
Goodrington Holiday Cen. TQ4: Good 1F **25**
Goodrington Orchard *TQ4: Good . . . . .3F 25* *(off Hookhills Rd.)*
Goodrington Rd. TQ4: Good 4D **24**
Goodrington Station
Dartmouth Steam Railway 1F **25**
Goodstone Way TQ4: Paig 2C **24**
Gorway TQ14: Teignm 3E **9**
Goshen Rd. TQ2: Torq 4H **19**
Gothic Rd. TQ12: New A 3G **11**
Gould Rd. TQ8: Salc 2G **35**
Gourders La. TQ12: Kingsk 5G **15**
Grace Gdns. TQ14: Teignm 3C **8**
Grafton Ct. *TQ1: Torq . . . . .5C 20* *(off Grafton Rd.)*
Grafton Hgts. TQ1: Torq 4D **20**
Grafton Rd. TQ1: Torq 5C **20**
TQ12: New A 2G **11**
Grafton Ter. TQ1: Torq 5C **20**
Graham Rd. TQ3: Pres 2D **22**
Gramercy Flds. TQ5: Brixh 5C **28**
Grampian Cl. TQ4: Coll M 1A **24**
Grandison Av. TQ14: Bi'ton 5H **9**
Grand Pier, The 5E **9**
Grand Prix Go Karts
Dawlish Warren 1H **3**
Paignton 2F **25**
Grange Av. TQ4: Good 3E **25**
Grange Cl. TQ12: New A 4A **12**
Grange Ct. Holiday Cen. TQ4: Good 2E **25**
Grange Dr. TQ14: Teignm 3D **8**
Grange Hgts. TQ4: Good 3D **24**
Grange Hgts. Cl. TQ4: Good . . .3D **24**
Grange Pk. TQ14: Bi'ton 5F **9**
Grange Pk. Caravan Pk. TQ12: A'well 1B **14**
Grange Rd. TQ1: Torq 4D **20**
TQ4: Good 4D **24**
TQ11: Buck 2A **32**
TQ12: A'well 1C **14**
Grange Vw. TQ4: Good 3D **24**
TQ12: A'well 1C **14**
Grasmere Cl. TQ2: Torq 5G **17**
Great Bridge TQ13: Ashb 3E **33**
Great Cliff EX7: Daw 5E **3**
Great Furlong TQ14: Bi'ton 5F **9**
Great Ga. La. *TQ3: Paig . . . . .5E 23* *(off Littlegate Rd.)*
Gt. Headland Cres. TQ3: Pres 2F **23**
Gt. Headland Rd. TQ3: Pres 2F **23**
Great Hill Rd. TQ2: Torq 3E **17**
Grea Tor Cl. TQ3: Pres 2C **22**
Great Pk. Cl. TQ14: Bi'ton 6G **9**
Greatpark La. TQ3: Paig 5A **22**
Gt. Parks Rd. TQ3: Paig 6B **22**
Gt. Rea Rd. TQ5: Brixh 2E **29**
Gt. Western Cl. TQ4: Good 1E **25**
Gt. Western Rd. TQ4: Paig 5E **23**
Greebys, The TQ3: Paig 5D **22**
Green, The *TQ13: Ashb . . . . .4F 33* *(off St Andrews Cl.)*
TQ14: Shal 6C **8**
Greenaway La. TQ12: Coff 1A **16**
Greenaway Rd. TQ12: New A . . .1F **11**
Greenbank TQ8: Bat 1G **35**
Greenbank Av. TQ12: Kingst 3E **7**
Greenbank Rd. TQ5: Brixh 3C **28**
Green Cl. TQ7: Kingsb 2C **34**
Greenfield Rd. TQ3: Pres 1D **22**
Greenhill TQ12: Kingst 5F **7**
Greenhill Gdns. TQ12: Kingsk . . .3G **15**
Greenhill La. TQ12: Den 6A **10**
Greenhill Rd. TQ12: Kingsk 3G **15**
TQ12: Kingst 5F **7**
Greenhill Way TQ12: Kingst 5E **7**
Greenlands Av. TQ3: Paig 5C **22**
Green La. TQ5: Chur F 2H **27**
TQ9: Tot 6E **31**
Greenover Cl. TQ5: Brixh 4C **28**
Greenover Rd. TQ5: Brixh 4C **28**
Green Pk. Rd. TQ3: Pres 2C **22**
Green Pk. Wlk. TQ3: Pres 2C **22**
Greenswood Rd. TQ5: Brixh 4D **28**
Greenway 5B **26**
Greenway Cl. TQ2: Torq 6F **17**
Greenway Gdns. TQ2: Torq 5F **17**
Greenway La. TQ1: Torq 1C **20**
Greenway Pk. TQ5: Galm 3E **27**
Greenway Rd. TQ1: Torq 1C **20**
TQ2: Torq 5G **19**
TQ5: Galm 5B **26**
Grenadine Cl. TQ2: Torq 4D **16**
Grendon Ct. TQ14: Teignm 4C **8**
Grenville Av. TQ2: Torq 3G **19**
TQ14: Teignm 2C **8**
Grenville Cl. TQ6: Dartm 4A **30**
TQ12: New A 2B **12**
Grenville Rd. TQ8: Salc 3G **35**
Grenville Way TQ4: Good 3E **25**
Greycoat La. TQ12: New A 4A **6**
Greystone Way TQ1: Torq 2C **20**
Groper's La. TQ3: Comp 1A **18**
Grosvenor Av. TQ2: Torq 6B **16**
Grosvenor Cl. TQ2: Torq 6B **16**
Grosvenor Rd. TQ4: Paig 6E **23**
Grosvenor Ter. TQ4: Paig 6E **23**
TQ14: Teignm 3D **8**
Grove, The TQ4: Paig 2B **24**
TQ9: Tot 4F **31**
Grove Av. TQ14: Teignm 4D **8**
Grove Cl. TQ9: Tot 4F **31**
Grove Ct. EX7: Daw 4F **3**
TQ14: Teignm 3E **9**
Grove Cres. TQ14: Teignm 4D **8**
Grove M. *TQ9: Tot . . . . .4F 31* *(off Grove Cl.)*
Grove Ter. TQ14: Teignm 4D **8**
Guardhouse Visitor Centre, The . . . . *2H 29* *(within Berry Head Country Pk.)*
Guestland Rd. TQ1: Torq 2D **20**
Guildhall Yd. TQ9: Tot 4F **31**
Gurneys, The TQ3: Paig 6D **22**

H

Haccombe Path TQ12: New A . . .3C **12**
Haccombe Rd. TQ12: Hacc, Neth 2F **13**
Hackney La. TQ12: Kingst . . . . . .5G **7** (not continuous)
TQ12: Neth 6H **7**
Hackney Marshes
Local Nature Reserve 6F **7**
Haddon Ct. *TQ3: Paig . . . . .4E 23* *(off Cecil Rd.)*
Hadfield Ct. TQ13: Chud K 1H **5**
Halcyon Rd. TQ12: New A 2G **11**
Haldon Av. TQ14: Teignm 3E **9**
Haldon Cl. TQ1: Torq 5F **21**
TQ12: New A 3C **12**
Haldon Ho. *TQ1: Torq . . . . .6G 17* *(off Teignmouth Rd.)*
Haldon Ri. TQ12: New A 3C **12**
Haldon Rd. TQ1: Torq 5E **21**
Haldon Ter. *EX7: Daw . . . . .4D 2* *(off High St.)*
Halfmoon Ct. TQ11: B'leigh 6A **32**
Hall La. EX7: Holc 1G **9**
Hall's La. TQ12: Kingsk 3G **15**
Halsteads Rd. TQ2: Torq 5F **17**
Hambleton Way TQ4: Paig 3D **24**
Hameldown Cl. TQ2: Torq 2E **19**
Hameldown Way TQ12: New A 1A **12**
Hamelin Way TQ2: Torq 2C **18**
TQ3: Marl 2C **18**
Hamilton Dr. TQ12: New A 1G **11**
Hamiltons, The TQ14: Shal 6C **8**
Ham La. TQ6: Ditt 4A **26**
TQ14: Shal 6B **8**
Hamlyns Way TQ11: B'leigh 4B **32**
Hampton Av. TQ1: Torq 1D **20**
Hampton Cl. TQ1: Torq 1D **20**
Hampton La. TQ1: Torq 1D **20**
Hampton Rd. TQ12: New A 2H **11**
Handley Ct. EX7: Holc 1H **9**
Hanover Cl. TQ5: Brixh 4D **28**
Hanover Ho. TQ1: Torq 6E **21**
Happaway Cl. TQ2: Torq 5F **17**
Happaway Rd. TQ2: Torq 5E **17**
Harberton Cl. TQ4: Paig 2B **24**
Harbour, The *TQ4: Paig . . . . .6F 23* *(off Roundham Rd.)*
Harbourne Av. TQ4: Paig 2B **24**
Harbour Vw. Cl. TQ5: Brixh 2D **28**
Hardy Cl. TQ1: Torq 6E **21**
Hares La. TQ13: Ashb 4F **33**
Harewood *TQ1: Torq . . . . .2D 20* *(off Cary Pk.)*
Harlington Ct. TQ12: New A 1H **11**
Harper's Hill TQ9: Tot 4E **31**
Harpins Ct. TQ12: Kingsk 1H **15**
Hartland Tor Cl. TQ5: Brixh 5B **28**
Hartley Rd. TQ4: Paig 6D **22**
Hartop Rd. TQ1: Torq 6G **17**
Harts Cl. TQ14: Teignm 3C **8**
Harwin Apartments TQ4: Good 1F **25**
Haslam Ct. TQ1: Torq 2B **20**
Haslam Rd. TQ1: Torq 2B **20**
Hatchcombe La. TQ2: Torq 5E **17**
Hatcher St. EX7: Daw 4D **2**
Hatfield TQ1: Torq 3C **20**
Hatfield Rd. TQ1: Torq 3C **20**
Hauley Rd. TQ6: Dartm 2B **30** (4C **30**)
Havelock Rd. TQ1: Torq 6G **17**
Haven, The TQ14: Bi'ton 5G **9**
Hawkes Way TQ9: Tot 4F **31**
Hawkins Av. TQ2: Torq 2F **19**
Hawkins Dr. TQ14: Teignm 3D **8**
Hawkins Rd. TQ12: New A 2C **12**
Hawthorn Cl. TQ7: Kingsb 4B **34**
TQ12: New A 5C **12**
Hawthorn Pk. Cl. TQ2: Torq 6G **19**
Haycock La. TQ5: Brixh 2F **29**
Hayes, The TQ5: Chur F 2H **27**
Hayes Cl. TQ9: Tot 5H **31**
Hayes Ct. TQ4: Paig 6C **22**
Hayes Gdns. TQ4: Paig 1D **24**
Hayes Rd. TQ4: Paig 1C **24**
Hayle Av. TQ4: Good 5E **25**
Hayley Pk. TQ12: Kingsk 4G **15**
Haytor Av. TQ4: Paig 3C **24**
Haytor Cl. TQ14: Teignm 3B **8**
Haytor Dr. TQ12: New A 2C **12**
Haytor Gro. TQ12: New A 2D **12**
Haytor Pk. TQ12: Kingst 4F **7**
Haytor Rd. TQ1: Torq 2C **20**
TQ13: Bov T 3A **4**
Haytor Ter. TQ12: New A 2G **11**
Haytor Vw. TQ12: Heat 3F **5**
Haywain Cl. TQ2: Torq 6A **16**
Hazel Cl. TQ7: Kingsb 4B **34**
TQ12: New A 4D **12**
TQ14: Teignm 1D **8**
Hazeldown Rd. TQ14: Teignm . . .2D **8**
Hazelwood *TQ1: Torq . . . . .4E 21* *(off Lwr. Warberry Rd.)*
Hazelwood Cl. TQ5: Brixh 3E **29**
Headborough Rd. TQ13: Ashb 3E **33**
Headland Gro. TQ3: Pres 2F **23**
Headland Pk. Rd. TQ3: Pres 2F **23**
Headland Rd. TQ2: Torq 1H **23**
Headlands, The TQ2: Torq 1H **23**
Headway Cl. TQ14: Teignm 4B **8**
Headway Cross Rd. TQ14: Teignm 3B **8**
Headway Ri. TQ14: Teignm 3B **8**
Heath Cl. TQ12: Heat 4F **5**
Heath Ct. TQ5: Brixh 1F **29**
TQ9: Tot 4F **31**
Heather Cl. TQ12: New A 1E **11**
TQ14: Teignm 2D **8**
Heatherdene TQ13: Bov T 3B **4**
Heather Est. TQ12: Heat 3E **5**
Heather Way TQ5: Brixh 3B **28**
HEATHFIELD 4E **5**
Heathfield Bus. Pk. TQ12: Heat 3E **5**
Heathfield Cl. TQ13: Bov T 5B **4**
Heathfield Cotts. TQ12: Heat 3F **5**
Heathfield Ho. *TQ13: Bov T . . . . .4B 4* *(off Ashburton Rd.)*
Heathfield Mdw. TQ13: Bov T . . .5B **4**
Heathfield Ter. TQ13: Bov T 4B **4**
Heath Hill TQ12: Heat 4F **5**
Heathlands Ct. *TQ14: Teignm . . . .1C 8* *(off Heathlands Ri.)*
Heathlands Ri. TQ14: Teignm 1C **8**
Heath Pk. TQ5: Brixh 2F **29**
TQ12: New A 4D **12**
Heath Ri. TQ5: Brixh 2F **29**
Heath Rd. TQ5: Brixh 2E **29**
Heath Way TQ9: Tot . . . . .4F **31** (not continuous)
Heatree Cl. TQ14: Teignm 1D **8**
Heaviside Cl. TQ2: Torq 4G **17**

Hele—Jordan St.

HELE . . . 6E 17
Hele Cl. TQ2: Torq . . . 6E 17
Helens Mead Cl. TQ2: Torq . . . 3F 17
Helens Mead Rd.
TQ2: Torq . . . 3F 17
Hele Pk. Golf Course . . . 1B 10
Hele Rd. TQ2: Torq . . . 6D 16
TQ12: Kingst . . . 2E 7
Helford Dr. TQ4: Good . . . 5E 25
Helford Wlk. TQ4: Good . . . 5E 25
Heligan Dr. TQ3: Paig . . . 3B 22
Hellevoetsluis Way
TQ3: Marl . . . 6B 18
Helmdon Ri. TQ2: Torq . . . 1E 19
Helston Cl. TQ3: Paig . . . 4C 22
Heltor Bus. Pk. TQ12: Heat . . . 2E 5
Hembury Cock Hill
TQ11: B'leigh . . . 2A 32
Hembury Pk. TQ11: Buck . . . 2B 32
Hems Brook Ct. TQ2: Torq . . . 1E 19
Henacre La. TQ7: Kingsb . . . 3D 34
Henacre Rd. TQ7: Kingsb . . . 3C 34
Henbury Cl. TQ1: Torq . . . 3C 20
Hennapyn Rd. TQ2: Torq . . . 6H 19
Hennock Rd. TQ4: Paig . . . 3C 24
Hensford Rd. EX7: Daw . . . 1C 2
Henty Av. EX7: Daw . . . 3F 3
Henty Cl. EX7: Daw . . . 2F 3
Herbert Rd. TQ2: Torq . . . 5G 19
TQ8: Salc . . . 3F 35
Hermitage Rd. TQ6: Dartm . . . 3A 30
Hermosa Gdns. TQ14: Teignm . . . 4D 8
Hermosa Rd. TQ14: Teignm . . . 4D 8
Heron Way TQ2: Torq . . . 4B 16
Hesketh Cres. TQ1: Torq . . . 6E 21
Hesketh M. TQ1: Torq . . . 6E 21
Hesketh Rd. TQ1: Torq . . . 6E 21
Hestow Rd. TQ12: Kingst . . . 1F 7
Hewett Cl. TQ12: New A . . . 2D 12
Heywood Cl. TQ2: Torq . . . 2G 19
Heywood Est. TQ12: Kingst . . . 6E 7
Heywoods Cl. *TQ14: Teignm . . . 4E 9*
(off Heywoods Rd.)
Heywoods Rd. TQ14: Teignm . . . 4E 9
Highbury Rd. TQ1: Torq . . . 3C 20
Highcliff Ct. *EX7: Daw . . . 4E 3*
(off E. Cliff Rd.)
Highcliffe M. TQ4: Good . . . 1F 25
High Cl. TQ13: Bov T . . . 3D 4
Higher Audley Av. TQ2: Torq . . . 1A 20
Higher Bibbery TQ13: Bov T . . . 3D 4
Higher Brimley TQ14: Teignm . . . 3D 8
Higher Brimley Rd.
TQ14: Teignm . . . 4D 8
HIGHER BRIXHAM . . . 4D 28
Higher Broad Pk. TQ6: Dartm . . . 4A 30
Higher Brook St.
TQ14: Teignm . . . 4D 8
Higher Buckeridge Rd.
TQ14: Teignm . . . 2D 8
Higher Budleigh Mdw.
TQ12: New A . . . 2E 11
Higher Cadewell La.
TQ2: Torq . . . 6A 16
Higher Compton Barton
TQ3: Comp . . . 3B 18
Higher Coombe Dr.
TQ14: Teignm . . . 2C 8
Higher Copythorne
TQ5: Brixh . . . 3B 28
Higher Downs Rd. TQ1: Torq . . . 1D 20
Higher Dr. EX7: Daw . . . 2F 3
Higher Edginswell La.
TQ2: Torq . . . 2D 18
Higher Erith Rd. TQ1: Torq . . . 5E 21
Higher Exeter Rd.
TQ14: Teignm . . . 1C 8
Higher French Pk.
TQ12: New A . . . 2E 11
Higher Furzeham Rd.
TQ5: Brixh . . . 1D 28
HIGHER GABWELL . . . 1H 17
Higher Holcombe Cl.
TQ14: Teignm . . . 2E 9
Higher Holcombe Dr.
TQ14: Teignm . . . 1E 9
Higher Holcombe Rd.
TQ14: Teignm . . . 1E 9
Higher Kingsdown Rd.
TQ14: Teignm . . . 4B 8
Higher Lincombe Rd.
TQ1: Torq . . . 6E 21
Higher Mnr. Rd. TQ5: Brixh . . . 2D 28
Higher Mnr. Ter. *TQ3: Paig . . . 6D 22*
(off Manor Ter.)
Higher Mill La. TQ11: Buck . . . 2B 32
(not continuous)
HIGHER MORLEY . . . 2A 10
Higher Penn TQ5: Brixh . . . 4E 29
Higher Polsham Rd.
TQ3: Paig . . . 4E 23
Higher Queen's Ter.
TQ1: Torq . . . 4C 20
Higher Ramshill La.
TQ3: Blag, Paig . . . 3A 22
Higher Ranscombe Rd.
TQ5: Brixh . . . 3E 29
Higher Ringmore Rd.
TQ14: Shal . . . 6A 8
Higher Roborough
TQ13: Ashb . . . 3G 33
Higher Rydons TQ5: Brixh . . . 3B 28
Higher Sackery TQ12: C'head . . . 1G 13
Higher Sandygate
TQ12: Kingst . . . 1E 7
Higherside TQ6: Dartm . . . 2A 30
Higher Steps *TQ5: Brixh . . . 2D 28*
(off Higher St.)
Higher St. TQ5: Brixh . . . 2D 28
TQ6: Dartm . . . 1B 30 (4C 30)
TQ6: Kingsw . . . 4D 30
HIGHER TOWN . . . 4A 32
Higher Union La. TQ2: Torq . . . 4B 20
Higher Union Rd.
TQ7: Kingsb . . . 3B 34
Higher Warberry Rd.
TQ1: Torq . . . 4D 20
Higher Warborough Rd.
TQ5: Galm . . . 1E 27
Higher Warren Rd.
TQ7: Kingsb . . . 5D 34
Higher Westonfields
TQ9: Tot . . . 4H 31
Higher Woodfield Rd.
TQ1: Torq . . . 6D 20
Higher Woodway Cl.
TQ14: Teignm . . . 2E 9
Higher Woodway Rd.
TQ14: Teignm . . . 1D 8
HIGHER YALBERTON . . . 2A 24
Higher Yalberton Rd.
TQ4: Paig . . . 2A 24
Higher Yannon Dr.
TQ14: Teignm . . . 3C 8
Highfield Cl. TQ5: Brixh . . . 3B 28
Highfield Cres. TQ3: Paig . . . 5B 22
Highfield Dr. TQ7: Kingsb . . . 4C 34
Highgrove Pk.
TQ14: Teignm . . . 2E 9
High Ho. Cl. EX7: Daw . . . 3E 3
High Ho. La. TQ7: Kingsb . . . 4C 34
Highland Cl. TQ2: Torq . . . 3F 19
Highland Rd. TQ2: Torq . . . 3F 19
High St. EX7: Daw . . . 4D 2
TQ9: Tot . . . 4E 31
HIGHWEEK . . . 6A 6
Highweek Cl. TQ12: New A . . . 6A 6
Highweek Rd. TQ12: New A . . . 1F 11
(not continuous)
Highweek St. TQ12: New A . . . 2G 11
Highweek Village
TQ12: New A . . . 6A 6
Highweek Way TQ12: New A . . . 2G 11
Highwood Grange
TQ12: New A . . . 3G 11
(not continuous)
Hillbrook Ri. TQ9: Tot . . . 4H 31
Hillbrook Rd. TQ9: Tot . . . 4H 31
Hilldown TQ9: Tot . . . 4H 31
Hilldrop Ter. TQ1: Torq . . . 4C 20
Hiller La. TQ12: Neth . . . 3E 13
Hillesdon Rd. TQ1: Torq . . . 4C 20
Hillfield TQ9: Sto G . . . 6A 24
Hillmans Rd. TQ12: New A . . . 3H 11
Hill Pk. Cl. TQ5: Brixh . . . 3F 29
Hill Pk. Rd. TQ1: Torq . . . 2B 20
TQ5: Brixh . . . 3F 29
TQ12: New A . . . 1E 11
Hill Pk. Ter. TQ4: Paig . . . 6F 23
Hillrise TQ5: Galm . . . 2E 27
Hill Rd. TQ12: New A . . . 3G 11
Hillsborough *TQ1: Torq . . . 5C 20*
(off Hillesdon Rd.)
Hillside Camp TQ4: Good . . . 4E 25
Hillside Cl. TQ14: Teignm . . . 2B 8
Hillside Cotts. TQ12: A'well . . . 1B 14
Hillside Ct. TQ6: Dartm . . . 4B 30
Hillside Dr. TQ7: Kingsb . . . 4C 34
Hillside Rd. TQ3: Paig . . . 4C 22
TQ5: Brixh . . . 3D 28
Hillside Ter. *TQ3: Paig . . . 5D 22*
(off Colley End Pk.)
Hill Vw. EX7: Holc . . . 1G 9
Hill Vw. Ter. TQ1: Torq . . . 2B 20
Hilly Gdns. Rd. TQ1: Torq . . . 6G 17
Hilton Cres. TQ3: Pres . . . 1F 23
Hilton Dr. TQ3: Pres . . . 2F 23
Hilton Rd. TQ12: New A . . . 3H 11
Hind St. TQ13: Bov T . . . 2C 4
Hingston Rd. TQ1: Torq . . . 2D 20
HMP Channings Wood
TQ12: Den . . . 6A 10
Hodson Cl. TQ3: Paig . . . 4C 22
Hoile La. TQ9: Sto G . . . 5A 24
Holbeam Cl. TQ12: New A . . . 1D 10
Holbeam La. TQ12: E Ogw . . . 1A 10
Holborn Rd. TQ5: Brixh . . . 1D 28
HOLCOMBE . . . 1G 9
Holcombe Down Rd.
EX7: Holc . . . 6A 2
TQ14: Teignm . . . 6A 2
Holcombe Dr. EX7: Holc . . . 1H 9
Holcombe Rd.
EX7: Holc . . . 6C 2 & 2G 9
TQ14: Teignm . . . 2G 9
Holcombe Village EX7: Holc . . . 1G 9
Holdsworth Ho. TQ6: Dartm . . . 2A 30
Hollacombe La. TQ3: Pres . . . 2G 23
Hollam Way TQ12: Kingst . . . 3G 7
Hollands Rd. TQ14: Teignm . . . 5E 9
HOLLICOMBE . . . 1G 23
Hollington Ho. TQ1: Torq . . . 5E 21
Hollywater Cl. TQ1: Torq . . . 4E 21
Holman Cl. EX7: Daw . . . 2F 3
Holme Ct. TQ1: Torq . . . 4E 21
Holmes Rd. TQ12: Heat . . . 4E 5
Holne Moor Cl. TQ3: Paig . . . 4B 22
Holne Rd. TQ11: B'leigh . . . 2A 32
Holwell Rd. TQ5: Brixh . . . 3C 28
Holwill Tor Wlk. TQ4: Paig . . . 2C 24
Homebourne Ho. *TQ4: Paig . . . 6F 23*
(off Belle Vue Rd.)
Home Cl. TQ5: Brixh . . . 4D 28
Homecombe Ho. *TQ1: Torq . . . 1D 20*
(off St Albans Rd.)
Homelands Pl. TQ7: Kingsb . . . 2B 34
Homelands Rd. TQ7: Kingsb . . . 2B 34
Home Mdw. TQ9: Tot . . . 4F 31
Homepalms Ho. *TQ1: Torq . . . 3A 20*
(off Teignmouth Rd.)
Home Pk. TQ13: Ashb . . . 3F 33
Homers Cl. TQ12: Kingst . . . 5E 7
Homers Cres. TQ12: Kingst . . . 5E 7
Homers La. TQ12: Kingst . . . 5E 7
Homestead Rd. TQ1: Torq . . . 1B 20
Homestead Ter. TQ1: Torq . . . 1B 20
Hometeign Ho. *TQ12: New A . . . 1A 12*
(off Salisbury Rd.)
Homeyards, The *TQ14: Shal . . . 6C 8*
(off Commons Old Rd.)
Homeyards Botanical Gdns. . . . 6C 8
Honey La. TQ12: S'head . . . 1E 17
Honeysuckle Cl. TQ3: Paig . . . 3B 22
Honeywell TQ12: Kingst . . . 5F 7
Honeywell Rd.
TQ12: Kingst . . . 5F 7
Hoodown La. TQ6: Kingsw . . . 3D 30
Hookhills Dr. TQ4: Good . . . 4F 25
Hookhills Gdns.
TQ4: Good . . . 5E 25
Hookhills Gro. TQ4: Good . . . 4F 25
Hookhills Rd. TQ4: Good . . . 5E 25
Hook La. TQ5: Galm . . . 4D 26
Hoopern Ter. *EX7: Daw . . . 4D 2*
(off Stockton Rd.)
Hope Cl. TQ9: Tot . . . 4H 31
Hope's Cl. TQ14: Teignm . . . 3C 8
Hope Wlk. TQ9: Tot . . . 4H 31
Hopkins Ct. *TQ12: New A . . . 2H 11*
(off Hopkins La.)
Hopkins La. TQ12: New A . . . 2H 11
Horace Rd. TQ2: Torq . . . 5E 17
Horn Hill TQ6: Dartm . . . 1A 30
Horns Pk. TQ14: Bi'ton . . . 5F 9
Horse La. TQ14: Shal . . . 6D 8
Horsepool St. TQ5: Brixh . . . 4C 28
Horseshoe Bend TQ4: Good . . . 3F 25
Hosegood Way TQ12: Kingst . . . 4E 7
Hoskings Ct. TQ11: B'leigh . . . 4B 32
Hospital Hill EX7: Daw . . . 4D 2
Hospital La. TQ13: Ashb . . . 3G 33
(not continuous)
Hound Tor Cl. TQ4: Good . . . 6E 25
House of Marbles & Teign Valley Glass . . . 5B 4
Howard Cl. EX7: Daw . . . 4D 2
(Old Town St.)
EX7: Daw . . . 4C 2
(off Penfield Gdns.)
TQ2: Torq . . . 3G 19
TQ14: Teignm . . . 2C 8
Howard Ct. TQ14: Teignm . . . 2C 8
Howards Way TQ12: New A . . . 1C 12
Howton Rd. TQ12: New A . . . 6A 6
Hoxton Rd. TQ1: Torq . . . 4C 20
Hoyles Ct. TQ3: Paig . . . 3B 22
Hoyle's Rd. TQ3: Paig . . . 3B 22
Huccaby Cl. TQ5: Brixh . . . 5A 28
Humber La. TQ12: Kingst . . . 3G 7
TQ14: Teignm . . . 3G 7
Humpy, The EX7: Daw . . . 3C 2
Hunsdon Rd. TQ1: Torq . . . 5D 20
Huntacott Way TQ2: Torq . . . 1E 19
Hunter's Moon *TQ1: Torq . . . 5E 21*
(off Babbacombe Rd.)
Hunters Tor Dr. TQ4: Good . . . 6E 25
Hunterswell Rd.
TQ12: New A . . . 2F 11
Hurrell Ct. TQ7: Kingsb . . . 3B 34
Hurrell Rd. TQ7: Kingsb . . . 3B 34
Hutchings Way TQ14: Teignm . . . 3B 8
Hutton Rd. TQ3: Pres . . . 2D 22
Huxley Va. TQ12: Kingsk . . . 4G 15
Huxnor Rd. TQ12: Kingsk . . . 4G 15
Huxtable Hill TQ2: Torq . . . 5G 19
Hyde Rd. TQ4: Paig . . . 5E 23
Hyfield Gdns. *TQ1: Torq . . . 5C 20*
(off Grafton Rd.)
Hyperion TQ2: Torq . . . 1H 23

I

Iddesleigh Ter. EX7: Daw . . . 4E 3
Idewell Rd. TQ2: Torq . . . 5G 17
Ilbert Rd. TQ7: Kingsb . . . 3B 34
Ilford Pk. TQ12: New A . . . 6E 5
Ilsham Cl. TQ1: Torq . . . 4G 21
Ilsham Cres. TQ1: Torq . . . 5G 21
Ilsham Ho. TQ1: Torq . . . 4F 21
Ilsham Marine Dr. TQ1: Torq . . . 4G 21
Ilsham M. TQ1: Torq . . . 4F 21
Ilsham Rd. TQ1: Torq . . . 4F 21
Ilton Way TQ7: Kingsb . . . 3C 34
Imperial Ct. TQ1: Torq . . . 2D 20
Imperial M. *TQ12: New A . . . 2H 11*
(off Lemon Rd.)
Indio Rd. TQ13: Bov T . . . 4B 4
Innerbrook Rd. TQ2: Torq . . . 4H 19
Inverteign Dr. TQ14: Teignm . . . 4B 8
Inverteign Hgts. TQ14: Teignm . . . 3B 8
IPPLEPEN . . . 5B 14
Ipplepen Rd. TQ3: Marl . . . 5A 18
Isaac Gro. TQ2: Torq . . . 4E 17
Isaacs Rd. TQ2: Torq . . . 4E 17
Isambard Ct. TQ2: Torq . . . 4G 17
Isigny Rd. TQ7: Kingsb . . . 3B 34
Island Quay TQ8: Salc . . . 2H 35
Island St. TQ8: Salc . . . 2G 35
Island Ter. TQ8: Salc . . . 2H 35
Ivatt Rd. TQ6: Dartm . . . 4A 30
Ivy Ho. *TQ14: Teignm . . . 5D 8*
(off Ivy La.)
Ivy La. TQ6: Dartm . . . 1A 30
TQ14: Teignm . . . 5D 8

J

Jack's La. TQ2: Torq . . . 4E 17
Jacolind Wlk. TQ5: Brixh . . . 3E 29
Jacqueline Ho. *TQ9: Tot . . . 4F 31*
(off Ticklemore St.)
James Av. TQ3: Paig . . . 2B 22
Jasmine Gro. TQ3: Paig . . . 3B 22
Jawbones Hill
TQ6: Dartm . . . 2A 30 (4C 30)
Jellicoe Rd. TQ12: New A . . . 2C 12
Jellicoe Vs. TQ9: Tot . . . 4E 31
Jetty Marsh Local Nature Reserve . . . 6D 6
Jetty Marsh Rd. TQ12: New A . . . 6C 6
John Nash Dr. EX7: Daw . . . 5C 2
John's Av. TQ2: Torq . . . 1A 20
Jonida Cl. TQ1: Torq . . . 2B 20
Jordan Dr. TQ14: Teignm . . . 3B 8
Jordan Mdw. TQ13: Ashb . . . 3G 33
Jordan Orchard *TQ11: B'leigh . . . 4A 32*
(off Jordan St.)
Jordan St. TQ11: B'leigh . . . 4A 32

Joslin Ct.—Louville Cl.

Joslin Ct. TQ12: Kingst 3E 7
Jubilee Cl. TQ1: Torq 4C 20
TQ6: Dartm 4A 30
Jubilee Rd. TQ9: Tot 3H 31
TQ12: New A 2G 11
Jubilee Ter. TQ3: Paig 5D 22
Jurys Cnr. Cl. TQ12: Kingsk 3H 15

K

Keatings La. TQ14: Teignm 4C 8
Keats Cl. TQ14: Teignm 2B 8
Keep Gdns., The TQ6: Dartm . . .4B 30
Keep La. TQ6: Dartm . . .1A 30 (3B 30)
Kelland Cl. TQ3: Paig 5C 22
Kellett Cl. TQ13: Ashb 3G 33
Kellock Dr. TQ9: Tot 4E 31
Kelly Cl. TQ1: Torq 6D 20
Kelvin Ct. TQ1: Torq 6H 17
TQ5: Brixh 2E 29
Kemmings Cl. TQ4: Paig 4C 24
Kemp M. *TQ13: Ashb 4F 33*
(off Bull Ring)
Kendlewood Cl. TQ4: Paig 2C 24
Kenilworth TQ1: Torq 6E 21
Kennels Rd. TQ5: Chur F 4F 27
Kenneth Ct. TQ2: Torq 1F 19
Kenneth Ter. *TQ2: Torq 1F 19*
(off Kenneth Ct.)
Kensey Cl. TQ1: Torq 3F 21
Kenton Brook Ct. TQ2: Torq 1E 19
Kent's Cavern & Visitor Cen. 4F 21
Kent's La. TQ1: Torq 4F 21
Kent's Rd. TQ1: Torq 4F 21
Kenwith Dr. TQ7: Kingsb 3C 34
Kenwyn Rd. TQ1: Torq 3D 20
Kernou Rd. TQ4: Paig 5F 23
Kerria Cl. TQ3: Paig 3B 22
Kerswell La. TQ12: Coff 2H 15
Kestor Dr. TQ3: Pres 2D 22
Kestrel Ct. TQ1: Torq 1D 20
Keyberry Cl. TQ12: New A 4A 12
Keyberry Mill TQ12: New A 4A 12
Keyberry Pk. TQ12: New A 4A 12
Keyberry Rd. TQ12: New A 4A 12
Keysfield Rd. TQ4: Paig 6F 23
Killerton Cl. TQ3: Paig 4E 23
Kilmorie TQ1: Torq 6G 21
Kilmorie Cl. TQ1: Torq 6G 21
Kiln Cl. TQ13: Bov T 5B 4
Kilnford Rd. TQ12: Kingst 4G 7
Kiln Forehead La.
TQ12: Kingst 4G 7
Kiln Ho. TQ7: Kingsb 4C 34
Kiln Orchard TQ12: New A 2E 11
Kiln Path TQ5: Brixh 3D 28
Kiln Rd. TQ3: Marl 6A 18
TQ5: Galm 3D 26
TQ13: Bov T 5B 4
Kilworthy TQ1: Torq 1C 20
King Charles Bus. Pk.
TQ12: Heat 2E 5
Kingcome Ct. TQ11: B'leigh 4C 32
Kingfisher Cl. TQ2: Torq 5C 16
Kingsale Rd. TQ8: Salc 3F 35
Kings Arms Pas.
TQ7: Kingsb 3B 34
(off Fore St.)
King's Ash Rd. TQ3: Paig 2B 22
Kings Av. TQ3: Paig 4F 23
KINGSBRIDGE 3C 34
Kingsbridge Cookworthy Mus.
. . . . .2B 34
Kingsbridge Hill TQ9: Tot 5F 31
Kingsbridge La. TQ13: Ashb 4F 33
Kingsbridge La. M.
TQ13: Ashb 4E 33
(off Kingsbridge La.)
Kings Coombe Dr.
TQ12: Kingst 2F 7
Kings Cotts. TQ12: New A 2H 11
Kings Ct. TQ12: Kingsk 3G 15
TQ12: Kingst 5F 7
Kingsdale Ct. TQ2: Torq 5C 20
Kingsdown Cl. EX7: Daw 3E 3
TQ14: Teignm 4B 8
Kingsdown Cres. EX7: Daw 3E 3
Kingsdown Rd.
TQ14: Teignm 4B 8
King's Dr. TQ5: Brixh 3E 29
King's Dr., The TQ2: Torq 5A 20
Kingsgate Cl. TQ2: Torq 3G 17
Kingshurst Dr. TQ3: Paig 3E 23
KINGSKERSWELL 3G 15
Kingskerswell Rd. TQ2: Torq . . .4B 16
TQ12: Kingsk 6B 16
TQ12: New A 4A 12
Kingsland Dr. TQ4: Paig 1B 24
Kingsleigh Mnr. *TQ1: Torq 4D 20*
(off Lwr. Warberry Rd.)
Kingsley Av. TQ2: Torq 4E 17
Kingsley Ct. *TQ2: Torq 4E 17*
(off Kingsley Av.)
Kingsley Rd. TQ7: Kingsb 4B 34
Kingsley Sq. TQ2: Torq 4E 17
King's Mkt. TQ7: Kingsb 3B 34
Kings Mdw. TQ12: Kingsk 3G 15
Kings Orchard TQ9: Tot 4H 31
Kings Quay TQ6: Dartm 3C 30
Kings Rd. TQ3: Paig 4F 23
Kings Rydon Cl. TQ9: Sto G 5A 24
KINGSTEIGNTON 4F 7
Kingsteignton Rd.
TQ12: New A 2H 11
Kingsteignton Swimming Pool
. . . . .2E 7
Kingston Cl. TQ12: Kingsk 2H 15
Kingston La. TQ6: Dartm 4A 30
King St. EX7: Daw 4D 2
TQ5: Brixh 2E 29
TQ12: New A 2H 11
King's Wlk. EX7: Daw 5E 3
Kingswater Ct. TQ5: Brixh 2D 28
Kingsway TQ14: Teignm 4B 8
Kingsway Av. TQ4: Good 4D 24
Kingsway Cl. TQ4: Good 4D 24
TQ7: Kingsb 4B 34
Kingsway Ct. TQ4: Good 4D 24
Kingsway Dr. TQ4: Good 4D 24
Kingsway Pk. TQ7: Kingsb 4B 34
KINGSWEAR 4D 30
Kingswear Rd.
TQ5: Brixh, Hill 6H 27
Kingswear Station
Dartmouth Steam Railway
. . . . .4D 30
Kingswood Ct. *TQ4: Paig 6F 23*
(off Cleveland Rd.)
Kiniver Ct. TQ14: Teignm 2E 9
Kinlacey Ct. TQ1: Torq 5D 20
Kintyre Cl. TQ2: Torq 5D 16
Kirkham Ct. *TQ3: Paig 5D 22*
(off Colley End Rd.)
Kirkham House 5D 22
(off Cecil Rd.)
Kirkham St. TQ3: Paig 5E 23
Kirkstead Cl. TQ2: Torq 1H 19
Kistor Gdns. *TQ9: Tot 3F 31*
(off Castle St.)
Kittiwake Dr. TQ2: Torq 4B 16
Knapp Pk. Rd. TQ4: Good 3F 25
Knebworth Ct. TQ1: Torq 6H 17
Knick Knack La. TQ5: Brixh 4D 28
Knights Mead TQ13: Chud K 1H 5
Knowle Gdns. TQ7: Kingsb 2B 34
Knowle Ho. Cl. TQ7: Kingsb 2C 34
Knowle Rd. TQ8: Salc 2G 35
KNOWLES HILL 1G 11
Knowles Hill Rd.
TQ12: New A 1G 11

L

Laburnum Ct. TQ12: A'well 1C 14
Laburnum Rd. TQ12: New A 4B 12
Laburnum Row TQ2: Torq 3A 20
Laburnum St. TQ2: Torq 4A 20
Laburnum Ter. TQ12: A'well 6G 11
Lacy Rd. TQ3: Pres 2D 22
Ladies Mile EX7: Daw 3G 3
Lady Pk. Rd. TQ2: Torq 6G 19
Lady's Mile Touring & Caravan Pk.
EX7: Daw 1F 3
Lake Av. TQ14: Teignm 2C 8
Lakeland TQ12: A'well 1C 14
Lakes Cl. TQ5: Brixh 2B 28
Lakeside TQ8: Salc 2G 35
Lakeside Cl. TQ13: Bov T 6B 4
Lakes Rd. TQ5: Brixh 3B 28
Lake St. TQ6: Dartm . . .1A 30 (4C 30)
Lamacraft Cl. EX7: Daw 2F 3
Lamb, The TQ9: Tot 4E 31
Lambert Cl. EX7: Daw 2F 3
Lamb Pk. Cl. TQ12: Kingst 1F 7
Lammas La. TQ3: Pres 3C 22
Lancaster Dr. TQ4: Paig 3C 24
Lancaster Ho. *TQ4: Paig 6F 23*
(off Belle Vue Rd.)
Landmark Rd. TQ8: Salc 3E 35
Landscore Cl. TQ14: Teignm 4D 8
Landscore Rd. TQ14: Teignm 4C 8
Landscove Holiday Village
TQ5: Brixh 3G 29
Lands Rd. TQ5: Brixh 1G 29
Lane, The TQ6: Ditt 5A 26
Langaller Cl. TQ13: Bov T 5A 4
Langaller La. TQ13: Bov T 6A 4
Langdon Flds. TQ5: Galm 1E 27
LANGDON HOSPITAL 1E 3
Langdon La. EX7: Daw 1C 2
TQ5: Galm 2E 27
Langdon Rd. EX7: Daw 1C 2
TQ3: Pres 2F 23
Langford Cres. TQ2: Torq 4E 17
Langlands Cl. TQ4: Paig 1B 24
Langley Av. TQ5: Brixh 3D 28
Langley Cl. TQ5: Brixh 3D 28
Langridge Rd. TQ3: Paig 3B 22
Langs Rd. TQ3: Pres 3F 23
Langstone Cl. TQ1: Torq 2E 21
TQ12: Heat 4E 5
Lang Way TQ12: Ipp 5C 14
Lanherne EX7: Daw 4E 3
Lanhydrock Cl. TQ3: Paig 3A 22
Lansdowne Ct. TQ2: Torq 4A 20
Lansdowne La. TQ2: Torq 3A 20
Lansdowne Pk. TQ9: Tot 5H 31
Lansdowne Rd. TQ2: Torq 3A 20
Lapthorne Ind. Est.
TQ12: Ipp 4A 14
Larch Cl. TQ14: Teignm 1D 8
Larch Wlk. TQ2: Torq 1F 19
Larks Cl. TQ14: Shal 6B 8
Larksmead Cl. TQ12: E Ogw 4F 11
Larksmead Way
TQ12: E Ogw 4E 11
Laura Av. TQ3: Paig 3E 23
Laura Gro. TQ3: Pres 3C 22
Laura Pl. *TQ3: Paig 5D 22*
(off Well St.)
Laurel La. TQ14: Shal 6B 8
Laureston Rd. TQ12: New A 3H 11
Laurie Av. TQ12: New A 1E 11
Lauriston Cl. TQ2: Torq 4A 20
Lavender Cl. TQ5: Brixh 3B 28
Lawn Cl. TQ2: Torq 4E 17
Lawn Hill EX7: Daw 4E 3
Lawns End TQ14: Bi'ton 5F 9
Lawn Ter. EX7: Daw 4E 3
Laywell Cl. TQ5: Brixh 5C 28
Laywell Rd. TQ5: Brixh 4B 28
Lea, The
TQ14: Bi'ton, Teignm
. . . . .5H 9 & 3A 8
Lea Cliff Pk. EX7: Daw W 1H 3
Leader La. TQ3: Marl 1A 22
Leadstone Camping EX7: Daw . . .1H 3
Lealands TQ13: Bov T 4B 4
Lea Mt. TQ14: Bi'ton 5H 9
Lea Mt. Cl. EX7: Daw 5E 3
Lea Mt. Dr. EX7: Daw 5D 2
Lea Mt. Rd. EX7: Daw 5E 3
Leander Ct. TQ14: Teignm 5D 8
Lea Rd. TQ2: Torq 4G 17
Leat Cl. TQ12: Kingst 4F 7
Leat Ter. TQ12: Kingst 4F 7
Lea Va. Rd. TQ12: New A 2F 11
Leaze Rd. TQ12: Kingst 3E 7
Ledsgrove TQ12: Ipp 5C 14
Leechwell Ct. *TQ9: Tot 4F 31*
(off The Lamb)
Leechwell La. TQ9: Tot 4F 31
(not continuous)
Leechwell St. TQ9: Tot 4F 31
(not continuous)
Lee Ct. TQ5: Brixh 3F 29
Leeward La. TQ2: Torq 4D 16
Leigham Ct. EX7: Daw 4E 3
Leigham Ter. *TQ7: Kingsb 3B 34*
(off Fore St.)
Leighon Rd. TQ3: Paig 5F 23
Le Molay-Littry Way
TQ13: Bov T 3C 4
Lemon Ct. *TQ12: New A 2H 11*
(off Marsh Rd.)
Lemon M. *TQ12: New A 2H 11*
(off The Avenue)
Lemon Pl. TQ12: New A 2H 11
Lemon Rd. TQ12: New A 2H 11
Lethbridge Ct. *TQ12: New A 2H 11*
(off Courtenay Pk. Rd.)
Level, The TQ6: Ditt 5A 26
Leyburn Gro. TQ4: Paig 1D 24
Leyfield Wlk. EX7: Daw 3E 3
Ley La. TQ12: Kingst 3E 7
Leys Rd. TQ2: Torq 4G 19
Lichfield Av. TQ2: Torq 5F 17
Lichfield Cl. TQ5: Brixh 3B 28
Lichfield Dr. TQ5: Brixh 3B 28
Lidford Tor Av. TQ4: Paig 2B 24
Light La. TQ5: Galm 3E 27
Lime Av. TQ2: Torq 4A 20
Lime Gro. TQ7: Kingsb 3B 34
Lime Tree Wlk. TQ12: New A 4B 12
Linacre La. TQ12: Coff 1B 16
Linacre Rd. TQ2: Torq 4E 17
Lincoln Grn. TQ2: Torq 6F 17
Lincombe Dr. TQ1: Torq 5F 21
Lincombe Hill Rd. TQ1: Torq . . .5F 21
Linden Rd. EX7: Daw 5C 2
Linden Ter. TQ12: New A 2F 11
Lindfield Cl. TQ2: Torq 1A 20
Lindisfarne Way TQ2: Torq 5D 16
Lindridge Cl. TQ12: Kingst 1E 7
Lindridge Hill TQ12: Kingst 1F 7
Lindridge La. TQ12: Kingst 1E 7
(not continuous)
Lindridge Rd. TQ1: Torq 1D 20
Lindsay Rd. TQ3: Pres 1D 22
Lindthorpe Way TQ5: Brixh 3C 28
Linhay Bus. Pk. TQ13: Ashb . . .2H 33
Linhey Cl. TQ7: Kingsb 4C 34
Links, The TQ1: Torq 6H 17
Links Cl. TQ5: Chur F 1H 27
Lion Cl. TQ7: Kingsb 3B 34
Lisburne Cres. TQ1: Torq 5E 21
Lisburne Pl. *TQ1: Torq 5E 21*
(off Lisburne Sq.)
Lisburne Sq. TQ1: Torq 5E 21
Little Barton TQ12: Kingst 2F 7
Lit. Bossell La. TQ11: B'leigh . . .5B 32
Little Cl. TQ12: Kingst 2F 7
Littlefield TQ14: Bi'ton 5F 9
Littlefield Cl. TQ2: Torq 6C 16
Littlegate Rd. TQ3: Paig 5E 23
Little Hayes TQ12: Kingst 2F 7
Little Hill TQ8: Salc 2F 35
Littlejoy Rd. TQ12: New A 2A 10
Lit. Park Rd. TQ3: Paig 5D 22
Little Roborough TQ13: Ashb . . .3F 33
Little Theatre, The
Torquay 6E 21
Little Triangle *TQ14: Teignm 5E 9*
(off Triangle Pl.)
Lit. Week Cl. EX7: Daw 1F 3
Lit. Week Gdns. EX7: Daw 1F 3
Lit. Week La. EX7: Daw 1F 3
Lit. Week Rd. EX7: Daw 1F 3
LIVERMEAD 1H 23
Livermead Hill TQ2: Torq 1H 23
Living Coasts 6C 20
Livingstone Rd.
TQ14: Teignm 3E 9
Lloyd Av. TQ2: Torq 1G 19
Locarno Av. TQ3: Pres 2G 23
Locks Cl. TQ1: Torq 2E 21
Locks Hill TQ1: Torq 2E 21
Locksley Cl. TQ1: Torq 2C 20
Locksley Grange TQ1: Torq 2B 20
Logan Rd. TQ3: Paig 4F 23
Long Barton TQ12: Kingst 2F 7
Longcroft Av. TQ5: Brixh 4C 28
Longcroft Dr. TQ5: Brixh 4C 28
Longfield Av. TQ12: Kingst 4G 7
Longfield Dr. TQ8: Salc 2F 35
Longfields TQ7: W Alv 4A 34
Longford La. TQ12: Kingst 3F 7
Longford Pk. TQ12: Kingst 3F 7
Longlands EX7: Daw 4D 2
Long La. EX7: Daw 1B 2
TQ12: Hacc 3E 13
TQ14: Shal 6A 8
Longmead Rd. TQ3: Pres 2C 22
Longmead Wlk. TQ3: Pres 2C 22
Long Pk. TQ13: Ashb 2G 33
Longpark Hill TQ1: Maid 1H 17
Long Rd. TQ4: Paig 3A 24
Long Rydon TQ9: Sto G 5A 24
Longstone Rd. TQ4: Paig 1B 24
Long Wools TQ4: Broads 6G 25
Lonsdale Rd. TQ12: New A 3A 12
Lonsee Gdns. TQ12: Kingsk 2G 15
Lord Nelson Dr. TQ6: Dartm 4A 30
Lord's Pl. TQ1: Torq 3C 20
Loring Rd. TQ8: Salc 3G 35
Lorris Dr. TQ14: Teignm 3C 8
Louville Camp TQ5: Brixh 2G 29
Louville Cl. TQ4: Good 3F 25

Love La.—Milford Cl.

Love La. TQ3: Marl 5A **18**
(not continuous)
TQ13: Ashb 4F **33**
TQ14: Teignm 2F **9**
Love La. Cl. TQ3: Marl 5A **18**
Lovelane Cotts. TQ3: Marl 5A **18**
Loventor Cres. TQ3: Marl 1A **22**
Lwr. Audley Rd. TQ2: Torq 1A **20**
Lwr. Blagdon La. TQ3: Blag 5A **22**
Lwr. Brimley Cl. TQ14: Teignm . . .4E **9**
Lwr. Brimley Rd.
TQ14: Teignm 3E **9**
Lwr. Broad Pk. TQ6: Dartm 4A **30**
Lwr. Broad Path TQ9: Sto G 6B **24**
Lwr. Brook St. TQ14: Teignm 5E **9**
Lwr. Budleigh Mdw.
TQ12: New A 2E **11**
Lwr. Cannon Rd. TQ12: Heat 4E **5**
Lower Collapark TQ9: Tot 3E **31**
Lwr. Collins Rd. TQ9: Tot 3E **31**
Lwr. Congella Rd. TQ1: Torq . . .3D **20**
Lwr. Contour Rd.
TQ6: Kingsw 4D **30**
Lwr. Coombe Rd.
TQ12: Kingst 4G **7**
Lwr. Dawlish Water EX7: Daw . . .2A **2**
LOWER DEAN 6A **32**
LOWER DITTISHAM 5A **26**
Lower Dr. EX7: Daw 2F **3**
Lwr. Ellacombe Chu. Rd.
TQ1: Torq 3D **20**
Lwr. Erith Rd. TQ1: Torq 5E **21**
Lwr. Fairview Rd.
TQ6: Dartm 4B **30**
Lwr. Fern Rd. TQ12: New A 5C **12**
Lower Fowden TQ4: Broads 1G **27**
Lwr. French Pk. TQ12: New A . . .2E **11**
Lwr. Kingsdown Rd.
TQ14: Teignm 4B **8**
Lwr. Manor Rd. TQ5: Brixh 2D **28**
Lwr. Meadow Ri. EX7: Daw 4C **2**
LOWER NETHERTON 1E **13**
Lower Pk. TQ3: Paig 4D **22**
Lwr. Penns Rd. TQ3: Pres 2F **23**
Lwr. Polsham Rd. TQ3: Paig 4E **23**
Lwr. Rea Rd. TQ5: Brixh 2E **29**
LOWER SANDYGATE 1E **7**
Lower Sandygate
TQ12: Kingst 1E **7**
Lwr. Shirburn Rd. TQ1: Torq . . .2B **20**
Lower St.
TQ6: Dartm 2B **30** (4C **30**)
TQ7: W Alv 4A **34**
Lwr. Thurlow Rd. TQ1: Torq 3B **20**
LOWER TOWN 4C **32**
Lwr. Union La. TQ2: Torq 4B **20**
Lwr. Union Rd. TQ7: Kingsb 3B **34**
Lwr. Warberry Rd. TQ1: Torq . . .4C **20**
Lwr. Warren Rd. TQ7: Kingsb . . .5C **34**
Lwr. Woodfield Rd.
TQ1: Torq 6D **20**
Lwr. Yalberton Holiday Pk.
TQ4: Paig 4A **24**
Lwr. Yalberton Rd. TQ4: Paig . . .3A **24**
Lowley Brook Ct. TQ2: Torq 1E **19**
Loxbury Ri. TQ2: Torq 5G **19**
Loxbury Rd. TQ2: Torq 4G **19**
Lucerne TQ1: Torq 5E **21**
Lucius St. TQ2: Torq 4A **20**
Lulworth Cl. TQ4: Paig 3C **24**
Lummaton Cross TQ2: Torq 5F **17**
Lummaton Pl. TQ2: Torq 6G **17**
Lupton House 4H **27**
Luscombe Cl. TQ12: Ipp 6B **14**
Luscombe Cres. TQ3: Paig 5B **22**
Luscombe Hill EX7: Daw 4A **2**
Luscombe La. TQ3: Paig 3A **22**
Luscombe Rd. TQ3: Paig 4A **22**
Luscombe Ter. EX7: Daw 4D **2**
Lutyens Dr. TQ3: Paig 4A **22**
Luxton Rd. TQ12: E Ogw 5E **11**
Lydford Ho. *TQ12: New A 1A 12*
(off Hameldown Way)
Lydwell Pk. Rd. TQ1: Torq 3E **21**
Lydwell Rd. TQ1: Torq 3E **21**
Lyme Bay Rd. TQ14: Teignm 2E **9**
Lyme Vw. Cl. TQ1: Torq 2E **21**
Lyme Vw. Rd. TQ1: Torq 2D **20**
Lymington Rd. TQ1: Torq 2A **20**
Lyncombe Cres. TQ1: Torq 6F **21**
Lyncourt TQ1: Torq 6E **21**
Lyndale Rd. TQ12: Kingst 3E **7**
Lyndhurst Av. TQ12: Kingsk 2H **15**
Lyndhurst Cl. TQ12: Kingsk 2H **15**
Lyn Gro. TQ12: Kingsk 1G **15**
Lyngrove Ct. *TQ12: Kingsk 1G 15*
(off Moor Pk. Rd.)
Lynmouth Av. TQ4: Paig 3C **24**
Lynway Ct. TQ1: Torq 3C **20**
Lynwood TQ12: E Ogw 4E **11**
Lyte Hill Ct. *TQ2: Torq 4E 17*
(off Lyte Hill La.)
Lyte Hill La. TQ2: Torq 4E **17**
Lyte's Rd. TQ5: Brixh 3E **29**
Lytton Ho. *TQ2: Torq 5B 20*
(off St Luke's Rd. Sth.)

M

Mabel Pl. TQ4: Paig 6E **23**
McKay Av. TQ1: Torq 3A **20**
Mackrells Ter. TQ12: New A 3F **11**
Maddacombe Rd.
TQ12: Kingsk 3E **15**
Maddacombe Ter.
TQ12: A'well 3D **14**
Maddicks Orchard
TQ9: Sto G 6A **24**
Madeira Pl. TQ2: Torq 4B **20**
Madrepore Pl. *TQ1: Torq 4C 20*
(off Pimlico)
Madrepore Rd. TQ1: Torq 5C **20**
Magdalene Cl. TQ9: Tot 4F **31**
Magdalene Rd. TQ1: Torq 3A **20**
Magistrates' Court
Newton Abbot 2G **11**
Torquay 4B **20**
MAIDENCOMBE 1H **17**
Maidencombe Ho. TQ1: Torq . . .3H **17**
Maidenway La. TQ3: Paig 3C **22**
Maidenway Rd. TQ3: Paig 3C **22**
Main Av. TQ1: Torq 1B **20**
Main Rd. TQ8: Salc 3F **35**
Malderek Av. TQ3: Pres 2F **23**
Mallands Mdw. TQ12: A'well 6F **11**
Mallard Cl. TQ2: Torq 4C **16**
Mallock Rd. TQ2: Torq 4H **19**
Malt Ho., The TQ9: Tot 4G **31**
Malt Mill La. TQ9: Tot 3E **31**
Malvernleigh *TQ1: Torq 1C 20*
(off St Marychurch Rd.)
Manaton Tor Rd. TQ3: Pres 2C **22**
Mannings Mdw. TQ13: Bov T 3C **4**
Manor Av. TQ3: Pres 3F **23**
Manor Bend TQ5: Galm 2F **27**
Manor Cl. EX7: Daw 4D **2**
TQ12: A'well 6F **11**
TQ12: Kingsk 4H **15**
Manor Cotts. *TQ12: New A 2G 11*
(off Wolborough St.)
Manor Ct. *TQ12: Kingsk 4H 15*
(off Torquay Rd.)
Manor Cres. TQ3: Pres 3F **23**
Manor Dr. TQ12: Kingsk 4H **15**
Mnr. Farm Camp Site
TQ12: Dacc 3D **16**
Manor Gdns. TQ1: Torq 6F **21**
TQ3: Pres 3F **23**
TQ7: Kingsb 2C **34**
TQ12: A'well 1C **14**
TQ12: Kingsk 4H **15**
Manorglade Ct. TQ1: Torq 4E **21**
Manor Ho. TQ1: Torq 6F **21**
Manor Ho., The TQ9: Tot 3F **31**
Manor Ho. Apartments, The
TQ2: Torq 6H 19
(off Seaway La.)
Manor Orchard *TQ12: E Ogw 4C 10*
(off Garners La.)
Manor Pk. TQ7: Kingsb 2C **34**
Manor Rd. TQ1: Torq 1C **20**
TQ3: Pres 3F **23**
TQ5: Brixh 2D **28**
TQ12: A'well 6F **11**
TQ12: New A 2E **11**
TQ14: Bi'ton 5G **9**
Manor Row *EX7: Daw 4D 2*
(off Brook St.)
Manor Steps TQ5: Brixh 2D **28**
Manor St. TQ6: Ditt 5A **26**
Manor Ter. TQ3: Paig 6D **22**
TQ5: Brixh 2D **28**
Manor Va. Rd. TQ5: Galm 2F **27**
Manor Vw. TQ12: New A 2F **11**
Manor Way TQ9: Tot 4F **31**
Mansbridge Rd. TQ9: Tot 4H **31**
Manscombe Cl. TQ2: Torq 6G **19**
Manscombe Rd. TQ2: Torq 1G **23**
Mansion Ho. St. TQ6: Dartm . . .2B **30**
Maple Av. TQ13: Bov T 6B **4**
Maple Cl. TQ5: Brixh 5B **28**
TQ12: Kingst 5F **7**
TQ13: Chud K 1H **5**
Mapledene Cl. TQ9: Sto G 5A **24**
Maple Gro. TQ4: Good 3E **25**
Maple Rd. TQ5: Brixh 5B **28**
(not continuous)
Mapleton Cl. TQ12: New A 1E **11**
Maple Wlk. TQ2: Torq 1F **19**
Marble Ct. TQ1: Torq 2A **20**
Marcent Ho. TQ5: Brixh 4E **29**
Marcombe Rd. TQ2: Torq 4H **19**
Mardle Way TQ11: B'leigh 4B **32**
Mardle Way Ind. Est.
TQ11: B'leigh 4B **32**
Margaret Cl. TQ12: E Ogw 4E **11**
TQ12: Kingst 4F **7**
Margaret Gdns. TQ12: New A . . .3C **12**
Margaret Rd. TQ12: E Ogw 4E **11**
TQ12: Kingst 4F **7**
Marguerite Cl. TQ12: New A 1E **11**
Marguerite Way
TQ12: Kingsk 3H **15**
Marina Cl. TQ5: Brixh 2F **29**
Marina Ct. *TQ4: Paig 6F 23*
(off Roundham Rd.)
Marina Dr. TQ5: Brixh 2F **29**
Marina Rd. TQ5: Brixh 3F **29**
Marine Ct. TQ3: Pres 3F **23**
Marine Dr. TQ3: Pres 4F **23**
Marine Gdns. TQ3: Pres 3F **23**
Marine Mt. TQ1: Torq 6H **21**
Marine Palms TQ2: Torq 5B **20**
Marine Pde. EX7: Daw 5E **3**
TQ3: Pres 3G **23**
TQ14: Shal 6D **8**
Marine Pk. TQ3: Pres 4F **23**
Marine Pk. Holiday Cen.
TQ4: Good 3E **25**
Mariners Ct. *TQ14: Shal 6C 8*
(off Commons Old Rd.)
Mariners Way TQ3: Pres 2C **22**
Marine Ter. *TQ14: Teignm 5D 8*
(off Foresters Ter.)
Marine Wlk. TQ5: Brixh 1D **28**
Market, The TQ1: Torq 4C **20**
TQ6: Dartm 1A 30
(off Market St.)
Market Cl. TQ11: B'leigh 4A **32**
Market Sq.
TQ6: Dartm 1A **30** (4C **30**)
TQ12: New A 2G **11**
Market St. TQ1: Torq 4C **20**
TQ5: Brixh 2D **28**
TQ6: Dartm 1A **30** (4C **30**)
TQ8: Salc 2H **35**
TQ11: B'leigh 4B **32**
TQ12: New A 2G **11**
Market Wlk. TQ12: New A 2G **11**
Markham Ct. *TQ4: Paig 6E 23*
(off Dartmouth Rd.)
Marlborough Av. TQ1: Torq 4E **21**
Marlborough Pl.
TQ12: New A 1F **11**
Marlborough Ter. TQ13: Bov T . . .3A **4**
MARLDON 1A **22**
Marldon Av. TQ3: Paig 5D **22**
Marldon Cross Hill TQ3: Marl . . .6A **18**
Marldon Gro. TQ3: Marl 6A **18**
Marldon Rd. TQ2: Torq 2C **18**
TQ3: Paig 2B **22**
Marldon Way TQ3: Marl 6B **18**
Marlowe Cl. TQ2: Torq 2G **19**
Marnham Rd. TQ1: Torq 2C **20**
Marsh La. TQ13: Bov T 4B **4**
Marsh Path TQ13: Bov T 3B **4**
Marsh Rd. TQ12: New A 2H **11**
Marston Cl. EX7: Daw 3F **3**
Martinique Gro. TQ2: Torq 4E **17**
Mary St. TQ13: Bov T 2B **4**
Mashford Av. TQ6: Dartm 3A **30**
Mathill Cl. TQ5: Brixh 4C **28**
Mathill Rd. TQ5: Brixh 4C **28**
Matlock Ter. *TQ2: Torq 4B 20*
(off St Luke's Rd.)
Maudlin Dr. TQ14: Teignm 1D **8**
Maudlin Rd. TQ9: Tot 4F **31**
Maxstoke Ct. TQ1: Torq 4E **21**
Maxwell Ct. *TQ1: Torq 3A 20*
(off McKay Av.)
TQ12: New A 3A **12**
Mayfair Rd. TQ12: Ipp 5B **14**
Mayfield Cres. TQ12: New A 2E **11**
Mayflower Av. TQ12: New A 3C **12**
Mayflower Cl. EX7: Daw 4E **3**
TQ6: Dartm 3A **30**
Mayflower Dr. TQ5: Brixh 4D **28**
Mayor's Av.
TQ6: Dartm 1B **30** (4C **30**)
Mead Cl. TQ3: Paig 4E **23**
Meadfoot Cl. TQ1: Torq 5G **21**
Meadfoot Ct. TQ1: Torq 6D **20**
Meadfoot Cross *TQ1: Torq 6D 20*
(off Parkhill Rd.)
Meadfoot Grange TQ1: Torq 6D **20**
Meadfoot La. TQ1: Torq 6D **20**
Meadfoot Rd. TQ1: Torq 6D **20**
Meadfoot Sea Rd.
TQ1: Torq 6E **21**
Mead La. TQ3: Paig 4E **23**
Meadow Brook TQ9: Tot 4G **31**
Meadow Cl. TQ9: Tot 4H **31**
TQ12: Kingsk 1G **15**
Meadowcroft Dr. TQ12: Kingst . . .2E **7**
Meadow Halt TQ12: E Ogw 3F **11**
Meadow Pk. EX7: Daw 3C **2**
TQ3: Marl 6A **18**
TQ5: Brixh 2C **28**
TQ11: B'leigh 3D **32**
TQ12: Ipp 5C **14**
Meadow Ri. EX7: Daw 3C **2**
TQ14: Teignm 2B **8**
Meadow Rd. TQ2: Torq 6H **19**
Meadows, The TQ12: Kingst 5G **7**
Meadow Side TQ12: New A 2F **11**
Meadowside Holiday Cen.
TQ4: Good 4E **25**
Meadow Vw. TQ12: E Ogw 4E **11**
Mead Rd. TQ2: Torq 1G **23**
Mead Way TQ12: New A 5A **12**
Meadwood TQ1: Torq 6E **21**
Meavy Av. TQ2: Torq 2E **19**
Medway Rd. TQ2: Torq 5G **17**
Melbourne Cotts
TQ6: Dartm 2A **30**
Melcot Cl. TQ12: Kingst 4F **7**
Meldrum Cl. EX7: Daw 4E **3**
Mellons Cl. TQ12: New A 1C **10**
Mellons Wlk. *TQ12: New A 1C 10*
(off Mellons Cl.)
Mellows Mdw. TQ12: New A 2E **11**
Melville La. TQ2: Torq 5C **20**
Melville Pl. *TQ2: Torq 5C 20*
(off Melville St.)
Melville St. TQ2: Torq 5C **20**
Mena Pk. Cl. TQ4: Paig 3C **24**
Mendip Rd. TQ2: Torq 6F **19**
Merchants Cnr. *TQ12: New A 2A 12*
(off Quay Rd.)
Mere La. TQ14: Teignm 4E **9**
Merivale Cl. TQ14: Teignm 2E **9**
Merlin Cinemas
The Central Cinema 5C **20**
Merlin Way TQ2: Torq 5C **16**
Merrifield Rd. TQ11: B'leigh 3A **32**
Merritt Flats *TQ3: Paig 6D 22*
(off Merritt Rd.)
Merritt Rd. TQ3: Paig 6D **22**
Merrivale Cl. TQ2: Torq 3G **17**
Merryland Cl. TQ3: Pres 1E **23**
Merryland Gdns. TQ3: Pres 1E **23**
Merrywood TQ12: E Ogw 4E **11**
Metherell Av. TQ5: Brixh 4D **28**
Metherell Av. Ind. Est.
TQ5: Brixh 4D **28**
Mews, The EX7: Daw 4E **3**
Mews Gdns. TQ6: Dartm 1A **30**
Meyrick Rd. TQ1: Torq 2D **20**
Middle Budleigh Mdw.
TQ12: New A 2E **11**
Middle Lincombe Rd.
TQ1: Torq 6E **21**
Middle St. TQ5: Brixh 2D **28**
TQ14: Shal 6C **8**
Middle Warberry Rd.
TQ1: Torq 4D **20**
Midvale Rd. TQ4: Paig 6E **23**
Midway TQ12: Kingsk 1G **15**
Miglo Ind. Est. TQ4: Paig 2B **24**
MILBER 4B **12**
Milber La.
TQ12: Coff, New A 6D **12**
TQ12: New A 3D **12**
Milber Trad. Est.
TQ12: New A 4D **12**
MILE END 1D **10**
Mile End Rd.
TQ12: New A . . . . . .1D **10** & 6A **6**
Milford Cl. TQ14: Teignm 4C **8**

Mill, The—Old Teignmouth Rd.

Mill, The TQ12: New A 1H 11
Millbrook Pk. Rd.
TQ2: Torq 4H 19
Millbrook Rd. TQ3: Paig 5E 23
Mill Cl. TQ12: New A 1D 10
Mill Ct. EX7: Daw 4C 2
Mill Cres. TQ6: Dartm 3A 30
Mill End TQ12: Kingst 1F 7
Millers La. TQ9: Sto G 6A 24
Mill Hill TQ9: Sto G 6A 24
Mill Hill Ct. TQ9: Sto G 6A 24
Mill La. TQ2: Torq 4A 20
TQ3: Comp 6D 14
TQ3: Paig 4E 23
TQ5: Brixh 6B 28
TQ5: Galm 3C 26
TQ9: Tot 4G 31
TQ12: E Ogw 4C 10
TQ12: N Whil 5E 15
(not continuous)
TQ13: Ashb 3E 33
TQ14: Teignm 3B 8
Mill Leat TQ12: E Ogw 2A 10
Millmans Rd. TQ3: Marl 6A 18
Mill Mdw. TQ13: Ashb 3E 33
Mill Path *TQ13: Ashb 4F 33*
(off St Andrews Cl.)
Mill St. TQ7: Kingsb 3B 34
Mill Tail TQ9: Tot 4F 31
Millwood TQ13: Bov T 6B 4
Millwood Bus. Pk.
TQ12: New A 1B 12
Milton Cl. TQ5: Brixh 5C 28
Milton Cres. TQ5: Brixh 5C 28
Milton Flds. TQ5: Brixh 5B 28
Milton Ho. TQ12: New A 3H 11
Milton La. TQ6: Dartm 5A 30
Milton Pk. TQ5: Brixh 5C 28
Milton Rd. TQ12: New A 1G 11
Milton St. TQ5: Brixh 6B 28
Minacre La. TQ12: N Whil 6F 15
Mincent Cl. TQ2: Torq 4F 17
Mincent Hill TQ2: Torq 4F 17
Minden Rd. TQ14: Teignm 4D 8
Miners Cl. TQ13: Ashb 3G 33
Minerva Bus. Pk.
TQ12: New A 2A 12
Minerva Way TQ12: New A 2B 12
Mint Casino
Torquay 4B 20
Miranda Rd. TQ3: Pres 3C 22
Mitre Cl. TQ14: Bi'ton 5F 9
(not continuous)
Moat Hill TQ9: Tot 5F 31
Moles La. TQ3: Marl 1B 18
TQ12: Kingst, N Whil 1B 18
Monastery Rd. TQ3: Paig 5D 22
Monksbridge Rd. TQ5: Brixh . . .4C 28
Monks Orchard TQ12: A'well 1B 14
Monks Way TQ13: Bov T 1A 4
Montagu Cl. TQ7: Kingsb 2C 34
Montagu M. *TQ7: Kingsb 2C 34*
(off Montagu Cl.)
Montagu Rd. TQ7: Kingsb 3B 34
Monterey *TQ4: Good 4F 25*
(off Hookhills Rd.)
Monterey Cl. TQ2: Torq 6H 19
Monterey Pk. TQ12: New A 4C 12
Montesson Cl. TQ3: Paig 4A 22
Montesson Rd. TQ3: Paig 4A 22
Montpelier Ct. TQ3: Pres 2E 23
Montpellier Rd. TQ1: Torq 5C 20
Montpellier Ter. *TQ1: Torq 5C 20*
(off Montpellier Rd.)
Montserrat Ri. TQ2: Torq 4D 16
Moorashes *TQ9: Tot 4F 31*
(off Grove Cl.)
Moor Cl. TQ14: Teignm 2E 9
Moore Cl. TQ12: New A 5C 12
Moorhaven Cl. TQ1: Torq 2H 19
Moorhayes TQ13: Bov T 3C 4
Moorings, The *TQ4: Paig 6F 23*
(off Belle Vue Rd.)
TQ7: Kingsb 5C 34
Moorings Reach TQ5: Brixh 2E 29
Moorland Av. TQ12: Den 6A 10
Moorland Ga. TQ12: Heat 4F 5
Moorland Pk. Caravan Pk.
TQ13: Bov T 6C 4
Moorlands Cl. TQ12: New A 3C 12
Moorland Vw. TQ11: B'leigh 4A 32
TQ12: New A 3C 12
Moor La. TQ2: Torq 4F 17
TQ13: Bov T 5B 4
Moor La. Cl. TQ2: Torq 4F 17
Moor Pk. TQ12: Kingsk 1G 15
Moor Pk. Rd. TQ12: Kingsk 1G 15
Moor Rd. TQ12: Ipp 4A 14
Moors End TQ12: Kingst 4E 7
Moorsend TQ12: New A 1D 10
Moors Pk. TQ14: Bi'ton 6G 9
Moorstone Leat TQ4: Good 4F 25
Moor Vw. *TQ13: Bov T 5B 4*
(off Brimley Rd.)
Moorview TQ3: Marl 1A 22
Moor Vw. Dr. TQ14: Teignm 2B 8
Moorview End TQ3: Marl 1A 22
Moretonhampstead Rd.
TQ13: Bov T 1B 4
Morgan Av. TQ2: Torq 4B 20
Morgans Quay TQ14: Teignm 6D 8
Morin Rd. TQ3: Pres 3F 23
Morningside EX7: Daw 6C 2
TQ1: Torq 4F 21
(off Barrington Rd.)
Mortimer Av. TQ3: Pres 3E 23
Motehole Rd. TQ12: Ipp 5B 14
Moult Hill TQ8: Salc 5E 35
Moult Rd. TQ8: Salc 5E 35
Mount, The TQ2: Torq 3E 17
TQ5: Brixh 1D 28
TQ14: Teignm 3D 8
Mt. Boone
TQ6: Dartm 1A 30 (3B 30)
Mt. Boone Hill
TQ6: Dartm 1A 30 (3C 30)
Mt. Boone La.
TQ6: Dartm 1A 30 (3C 30)
Mt. Boone Way TQ6: Dartm 3B 30
Mt. Braddons M. TQ1: Torq 5D 20
Mt. Flagon Steps TQ6: Dartm . . .1A 30
Mt. Galpine
TQ6: Dartm 1A 30 (3C 30)
Mt. Hermon Rd. TQ1: Torq 3C 20
Mt. Pleasant Cl.
TQ7: Kingsb 2C 34
TQ12: Kingsk 4H 15
Mt. Pleasant La. TQ14: Shal 6C 8
Mt. Pleasant M. TQ5: Brixh 3D 28
Mt. Pleasant Rd.
EX7: Daw W 1G 3
TQ1: Torq 3C 20
TQ5: Brixh 3D 28
TQ12: Kingsk 4H 15
TQ12: New A 3H 11
Mount Rd. TQ5: Brixh 3E 29
MOUNT STUART PRIVATE HOSPITAL
. . . . .2A 20
Mount Vw. Ter. *TQ9: Tot 4F 31*
(off The Grove)
Mudstone La. TQ5: Brixh 4E 29
Mulberry Cl. TQ3: Paig 4B 22
Mulberry St. TQ14: Teignm 4D 8
Murley Cres. TQ14: Bi'ton 5F 9
Murley Grange TQ14: Bi'ton 5F 9
Museum Ct. TQ7: Kingsb 2B 34
Museum Rd. TQ1: Torq 5D 20
Musket Rd. TQ12: Heat 4E 5
Myrtle Hill TQ14: Teignm 4E 9

N

Naida Va. TQ6: Dartm 2C 30
Naseby Dr. TQ12: Heat 4E 5
Nash Gdns. EX7: Daw 6D 2
Nelson Cl. TQ14: Teignm 3C 8
Nelson Pl. TQ12: New A 6C 6
Nelson Rd. TQ5: Brixh 2D 28
TQ6: Dartm 3A 30
Nelson Rd. Ind. Est.
TQ6: Dartm 3A 30
(off Nelson Rd.)
Ness Dr. TQ14: Shal 6D 8
Ness Vw. Rd. TQ14: Teignm 1E 9
Netherleigh Rd. TQ1: Torq 2C 20
Nether Mdw. TQ3: Marl 6A 18
NETHERTON 2F 13
Netley Rd. TQ12: New A 1G 11
Neville Rd. TQ12: New A 1F 11
Newbury Dr. TQ13: Bov T 3D 4
Newcause *TQ11: B'leigh 4B 32*
(off Jordan St.)
Newcomen Engine House
. . . . .1B 30 (4C 30)
Newcomen Rd.
TQ6: Dartm 2B 30 (4C 30)
Newcross Pk. TQ12: Kingst 2D 6
New Esplanade Ct.
TQ3: Paig 5F 23
Newfoundland Way
TQ12: New A 2G 11
Newhay, The EX7: Daw 4C 2
Newhay Cl. EX7: Daw 4C 2
Newhayes TQ12: Ipp 6A 14
Newlands EX7: Daw 3E 3
Newlands Dr. TQ13: Bov T 6B 4
New Pk. TQ13: Bov T 6B 4
New Pk. Cl. TQ5: Brixh 3E 29
New Pk. Cres. TQ12: Kingst 3E 7
New Pk. Rd. TQ3: Paig 4C 22
TQ12: Kingst 3E 7
Newport St.
TQ6: Dartm 1A 30 (4C 30)
New Quay La. TQ5: Brixh 2E 29
New Quay St. TQ14: Teignm 5D 8
New Rd. TQ5: Brixh 3C 28
TQ9: Sto G 6A 24
TQ9: Tot 3G 31
TQ11: B'leigh 4B 32
TQ14: Teignm 3D 8
New St. TQ3: Paig 5E 23
NEWTAKE 4C 12
Newtake Ho. TQ2: Torq 6E 17
Newtake Mt. TQ12: New A 3C 12
Newtake Ri. TQ12: New A 4C 12
NEWTON ABBOT 2A 12
NEWTON ABBOT
COMMUNITY HOSPITAL . . .6C 6
Newton Abbot Leisure Cen. . . .1F 11
Newton Abbot Racecourse 6E 7
Newton Abbot Rd. TQ9: Tot 4G 31
Newton Abbot Sailing Club 4H 11
Newton Abbot Station (Rail) . . .2A 12
Newton Abbot Town &
Great Western Railway Mus.
. . . . .2H 11
Newton Hall TQ12: New A 3H 11
Newton Hill TQ12: S'head 1E 17
Newton Rd. TQ2: Torq 6B 16
TQ8: Salc 3G 35
TQ9: L'ton, Tot 3G 31
TQ12: Heat . . . . .5C 4 & 4E 5
TQ12: Kingsk 2H 15
TQ12: Kingst, New A 1H 11
TQ13: Bov T 3B 4
TQ14: Bi'ton 6F 9
Newton Rd. Retail Pk.
TQ12: Kingst 5E 7
New Wlk. TQ9: Tot 4G 31
Nicholson Rd. TQ2: Torq 5C 16
Nightingale Cl. TQ2: Torq 5D 16
Nightjar Cl. TQ2: Torq 5D 16
Noelle Dr. TQ12: New A 1F 11
Norden La. TQ7: Kingsb 3A 34
Norman Cl. TQ12: New A 6A 6
Normandy Way TQ8: Salc 2H 35
Norman Rd. TQ3: Paig 4F 23
Nth. Boundary Rd.
TQ5: Brixh 2B 28
North Embankment
TQ6: Dartm 1B 30 (3C 30)
North End Cl. TQ12: Ipp 5A 14
Northernhay TQ12: New A 3H 11
Northfields Ind. Est.
TQ5: Brixh 2C 28
Northfields La. TQ5: Brixh 2C 28
Northford Rd.
TQ6: Dartm 1A 30 (4B 30)
Nth. Furzeham Rd.
TQ5: Brixh 1D 28
Northgate *TQ9: Tot 3F 31*
(off Castle St.)
North Hill Cl. TQ5: Brixh 2C 28
Northleat Av. TQ3: Paig 6B 22
Nth. Lodge Cl. EX7: Daw 5C 2
Nth. Rocks Rd. TQ4: Broads 6E 25
North St. TQ9: Tot 3F 31
TQ12: Den 6A 10
TQ12: Ipp 5A 14
TQ13: Ashb 3E 33
Northumberland Pl.
TQ14: Teignm 5D 8
North Vw. *TQ14: Shal 6C 8*
(off Commons Old Rd.)
North Vw. Rd. TQ5: Brixh 2E 29
Northville Pk. TQ7: Kingsb 2B 34
Northville Rd. TQ7: Kingsb 2B 34
NORTH WHILBOROUGH 6F 15
Northwood La. TQ11: Buck 1B 32
Northwoods TQ13: Bov T 6B 4
Norton Vw. *TQ6: Dartm 4A 30*
(off Townstal Rd.)
Nursery Cl. TQ3: Paig 6D 22
Nursery Rd. TQ12: Kingst 4F 7
Nut Bush La. TQ2: Torq 2E 19
Nuthatch Dr. TQ2: Torq 5D 16
Nut Tree Ct. TQ5: Brixh 5C 28
Nut Tree Orchard TQ5: Brixh 5C 28

O

Oakbank TQ13: Bov T 6B 4
Oak Cliff Chalet Pk.
EX7: Daw W 1H 3
Oak Cliff Holiday Pk.
EX7: Daw W 1H 3
Oak Cl. TQ12: Kingst 5G 7
Oak End Ct. TQ3: Marl 1A 22
Oakford TQ12: Kingst 4E 7
Oak Hill EX7: Daw 6C 2
Oak Hill Cross Rd.
EX7: Holc . . . . .2F 9 & 6B 2
TQ14: Teignm 2F 9
Oak Hill Rd. TQ1: Torq 3A 20
Oakland Dr. EX7: Daw 5D 2
Oakland Rd. TQ12: New A 3B 12
Oaklands Cl. TQ11: B'leigh 4A 32
Oaklands Pk. TQ11: B'leigh 3A 32
Oaklands Rd. TQ11: B'leigh 3A 32
Oakland Wlk. EX7: Daw 5D 2
Oak Lawn TQ12: New A 3H 11
Oaklawn Ct. *TQ1: Torq 2A 20*
(off Barton Rd.)
Oaklawn Ter. *TQ1: Torq 2A 20*
(off St Vincent's Rd.)
Oaklea Cl. TQ7: Kingsb 4B 34
Oakley Cl. TQ14: Teignm 2D 8
Oak Pk. Av. TQ2: Torq 1G 19
Oak Pk. Cl. TQ2: Torq 1G 19
Oak Pk. Rd. TQ12: New A 1E 11
Oak Pk. Vs. EX7: Daw 3E 3
Oak Pl. TQ12: New A 2H 11
(not continuous)
Oaks, The TQ12: New A 5C 12
TQ13: Bov T 3D 4
Oak Tree Dr. TQ12: New A 5C 12
Oak Tree Gro. TQ14: Shal 6C 8
Oak Vw. Cl. TQ2: Torq 6A 16
Oakwood Cl. *TQ6: Dartm 4A 30*
(off Townstal Rd.)
Oakymead Pk. TQ12: Kingst 5E 7
Oatlands Dr. TQ4: Paig 1D 24
Occombe Farm 6B 18
Occombe Valley Rd.
TQ3: Pres 1D 22
Ocean Vw. Cres. TQ5: Brixh 6B 28
Ocean Vw. Dr. TQ5: Brixh 6B 28
Ochre Ct. TQ5: Brixh 3E 29
Octon Gro. TQ1: Torq 2H 19
Oddicombe Beach Hill
TQ1: Torq 1D 20
Odle Hill TQ12: A'well 6F 11
Odlehill Gro. TQ12: A'well 1B 14
Ogwell End Dr. TQ12: E Ogw . . .3E 11
Ogwell Grn. TQ12: E Ogw 4D 10
Ogwell Mill Rd.
TQ12: New A 3D 10
Ogwell Rd. TQ12: E Ogw 4D 10
Oke Tor Cl. TQ3: Pres 1D 22
Old Brewery, The *TQ2: Torq 6G 17*
(off Lummaton Pl.)
Old Cider Works La.
TQ12: A'well 6F 11
Oldenburg Pk. TQ3: Paig 4F 23
Old Exeter Rd. TQ12: New A . . .1G 11
TQ13: Ashb 2H 33
Old Farm Way EX7: Daw 6D 2
Old Gatehouse Rd. EX7: Daw 3E 3
Old Market, The *TQ6: Dartm . . .1A 30*
(off Market St.)
Old Mill La. TQ6: Dartm 3A 30
Old Mill Rd. TQ2: Torq 1H 23
(not continuous)
Old Newton Rd. TQ12: Heat 5C 4
TQ12: Kingsk 1F 15
TQ13: Bov T 5C 4
Old Orchard TQ13: Bov T 3C 4
Old Paignton Rd. TQ2: Torq 1G 23
(Roundhill Rd.)
TQ2: Torq 6G 19
(Stoneleigh Dr.)
Old Quay TQ14: Teignm 5D 8
Old Quay St. TQ14: Teignm 5D 8
Old Rd. TQ5: Galm 2E 27
Old School M. *EX7: Daw 4D 2*
(off School Hill)
Old Station Yd. TQ7: Kingsb 3B 34
Old Teignmouth Rd. EX7: Daw . . .6D 2

Old Torquay Rd.—Princess Theatre

Old Torquay Rd. TQ3: Pres 3F **23**
Old Torwood Rd. TQ1: Torq 5D **20**
Old Totnes Rd. TQ11: B'leigh . . .4C **32**
TQ12: New A 3F **11**
(not continuous)
TQ13: Ashb 5E **33**
Old Town St. EX7: Daw 4C **2**
Old Walls Hill
TQ14: Bi'ton, Teignm 1A **8**
OLDWAY 4E **23**
Oldway Mansion 3E **23**
Oldway Rd. TQ3: Paig, Pres 4E **23**
Old Widdicombe La.
TQ3: Paig 4A **22**
Old Woods Hill TQ2: Torq 2H **19**
Old Woods Trad. Est.
TQ2: Torq 1H **19**
Oliver Pl. TQ12: Heat 4F **5**
Onslow Rd. TQ8: Salc 2F **35**
Orange Gro. TQ2: Torq 5F **17**
Orbec Av. TQ12: Kingst 4G **7**
Orchard, The EX7: Holc 1G **9**
TQ9: Tot 4G ***31***
(off Shute Rd.)
TQ11: B'leigh 4C **32**
TQ12: A'well 1C **14**
TQ14: Bi'ton 5G **9**
Orchard Cl. EX7: Daw 4D **2**
TQ5: Brixh 4D **28**
TQ5: Galm 2F **27**
TQ9: Sto G 6A ***24***
(off Paignton Rd.)
TQ12: E Ogw 4C **10**
TQ12: Kingst 1E **7**
(The Villas)
TQ12: Kingst 4G **7**
(Ware Cl.)
TQ14: Shal 6B **8**
Orchard Ct. *TQ8: Salc 2G* ***35***
(off Island St.)
TQ12: New A 2G ***11***
(off Bradley La.)
Orchard Dr. TQ12: Ipp 5B **14**
TQ12: Kingsk 3G **15**
Orchard Gdns. EX7: Daw 4D **2**
TQ6: Dartm 4B **30**
TQ12: Kingst 4F ***7***
(off Crossley Moor Rd.)
TQ14: Teignm 5E **9**
Orchard Gro. TQ5: Brixh 5D **28**
Orchard Ind. Est. (North)
TQ7: Kingsb 3B **34**
Orchard Ind. Est. (South)
TQ7: Kingsb 3B **34**
Orchard Pl. TQ1: Torq 6E **21**
Orchard Rd. TQ1: Torq 3C **20**
TQ2: Torq 6E **17**
TQ13: Ashb 4F **33**
Orchards, The TQ5: Galm 2E **27**
Orchard Ter. TQ9: Tot 4F **31**
TQ11: B'leigh 4B **32**
TQ12: A'well 6G **11**
TQ12: Kingsk 2G **15**
TQ13: Bov T 2C **4**
Orchard Way TQ2: Torq 6A **16**
TQ9: Sto G 5A **24**
TQ13: Bov T 2C **4**
Orchard Waye TQ9: Tot 4E **31**
Orchid Av. TQ12: Kingst 4F **7**
Orchid Paradise 4A **6**
Orchid Va. TQ12: Kingst 2F **7**
Orestone Dr. TQ1: Maid 2H **17**
Orestone La. TQ12: Dacc 4C **16**
Orient Rd. TQ3: Pres 2G **23**
Orkney Cl. TQ2: Torq 5D **16**
Orleigh Av. TQ12: New A 6C **6**
Orleigh Cross TQ12: New A 6C **6**
Orleigh Pk. TQ12: New A 6C **6**
Orley Rd. TQ12: Ipp 5A **14**
Ormond Lodge TQ4: Paig 6F **23**
Osbern Rd. TQ3: Pres 1D **22**
Osborn Cl. TQ12: Ipp 5B **14**
Osborne St. TQ12: New A 2A **12**
Osmonds La. TQ14: Teignm 5D **8**
Osney Av. TQ4: Good 1E **25**
Osney Cres. TQ4: Good 6E **23**
Osney Gdns. TQ4: Good 1E **25**
Osprey Dr. TQ2: Torq 4C **16**
Osprey Ho. *TQ1: Torq 2E* ***21***
(off Babbacombe Rd.)
Otter Cl. TQ2: Torq 2F **19**
Otter Rd. TQ2: Torq 2F **19**
Outlook Ct. *EX7: Daw 4E* ***3***
(off E. Cliff Rd.)
Overbeck's 6E **35**
Overbrook EX7: Daw 4C **2**
Overcliff Ct. EX7: Daw 3E **3**
Overclose TQ3: Paig 3B **22**
Overdale Cl. TQ2: Torq 3E **17**
Overgang TQ5: Brixh 2E **29**
Overgang Rd. TQ5: Brixh 1D **28**
Oxenham Grn. TQ2: Torq 3G **19**
Oxford Ct. TQ2: Torq 6E **17**
Oxford La. TQ5: Brixh 3B **28**
Oxford St.
TQ6: Dartm 2B **30** (4C **30**)
Oxlea Cl. TQ1: Torq 5F **21**
Oxlea Rd. TQ1: Torq 5F **21**
Oyster Bend TQ4: Good 3F **25**
Oystercatcher Ct. TQ14: Shal 6B **8**
Oyster Cl. TQ4: Good 3F **25**

P

Packhall La. TQ5: Brixh 5B **28**
(not continuous)
Padacre Rd. TQ2: Torq 3F **17**
Paddock, The EX7: Daw 3D **2**
Paddocks, The TQ9: Tot 3G **31**
TQ12: A'well 6G **11**
Paddons Coombe
TQ12: Kingst 2F **7**
Paddons La. TQ14: Teignm 2C **8**
Pafford Av. TQ2: Torq 5G **17**
Pafford Cl. TQ2: Torq 5F **17**
Paige Adams Rd. TQ9: Tot 3E **31**
PAIGNTON 5E **23**
Paignton & Dartmouth
Steam Railway Vis. Cen.
. . . . .4D **30**
PAIGNTON HOSPITAL 5E **23**
Paignton Pier 5G **23**
Paignton Rd. TQ9: Sto G 5A **24**
Paignton Sailing Club *6G* ***23***
(off South Quay)
Paignton Station
Dartmouth Steam Railway
. . . . .6E **23**
Paignton Station (Rail) 5E **23**
Paignton Zoo 1C **24**
Palace Av. TQ3: Paig 5E **23**
Palace Pl. TQ3: Paig 5E **23**
Palace Theatre 5E **23**
Palatine Cl. TQ1: Torq 4C **20**
Palermo TQ1: Torq 5E **21**
Palermo Rd. TQ1: Torq 2D **20**
Palk Cl. TQ14: Shal 6B **8**
Palk Pl. *TQ1: Torq 6G* ***17***
(off Teignmouth Rd.)
Palk St. TQ2: Torq 5C **20**
Palm Rd. TQ2: Torq 4B **20**
Palms, The TQ1: Torq 5E **21**
Panorama *TQ2: Torq 1H* ***23***
(off Livermead Hill)
Paradise Glen TQ14: Teignm 3D **8**
Paradise Pl. TQ5: Brixh 2D **28**
Paradise Rd. TQ14: Teignm 3D **8**
Paradise Wlk. TQ4: Good 1F **25**
Paris Rd. TQ3: Pres 3F **23**
Park & Ride
Brixham 2G **27**
Salcombe 2F **35**
Park Av. TQ5: Brixh 4C **28**
Park Ct. TQ5: Brixh 2F **29**
Parkelands TQ13: Bov T 3B **4**
Parkers Cl. TQ9: Tot 5G **31**
Parkers Way TQ9: Tot 5G **31**
Parkfield Cl. TQ3: Marl 6A **18**
TQ9: Tot 4H **31**
Parkfield Rd. TQ1: Torq 2A **20**
Park Hall TQ1: Torq 6D **20**
Parkham Glade TQ5: Brixh 3D **28**
Parkham La. TQ5: Brixh 3D **28**
Parkham Rd. TQ5: Brixh 3D **28**
Parkham Towers *TQ5: Brixh 3D* ***28***
(off Wren Hill)
Park Hill TQ14: Teignm 5D **8**
Parkhill Rd. TQ1: Torq 6C **20**
Parkhurst Rd. TQ1: Torq 2A **20**
Parkland Caravan Pk.
TQ4: Good 4D **24**
Parklands TQ9: Tot 3F **31**
Parklands Way TQ13: Bov T 6B **4**
Park La. TQ1: Torq 6C **20**
Park La. Steps *TQ1: Torq 6D* ***20***
(off Park La.)
Park M. TQ5: Brixh 2F **29**
Park Ri. EX7: Daw 5D **2**
TQ8: Salc 3F **35**
Park Rd. EX7: Daw 4D **2**
TQ1: Torq 6G **17**
TQ12: Kingsk 2G **15**
Parkside TQ8: Salc 2G **35**
Parkside Rd. TQ4: Paig 5F **23**
Parkside Vs. *TQ1: Torq 2D* ***20***
(off Palermo Rd.)
Park Vw. TQ12: New A 5C **12**
Parson St. TQ14: Teignm 4D **8**
Paternoster La. TQ12: Ipp 5A **14**
Pathfields TQ9: Tot 4G **31**
Pathfields Cl. TQ9: Tot 4G **31**
Pavilion, The TQ2: Torq 6C **20**
Pavilions Cl. TQ5: Brixh 2C **28**
Pavor Rd. TQ2: Torq 5G **17**
Paynsford M. TQ12: New A 1G **11**
Paynsford Rd. TQ12: New A 1G **11**
Peak Tor Av. TQ1: Torq 6D **20**
Peaseditch TQ5: Brixh 4E **29**
Peasland Rd. TQ2: Torq 3F **17**
Pebble Ct. TQ4: Good 1E **25**
Pegasus Ct. TQ3: Paig 3E **23**
Pellew Arc. *TQ14: Teignm 5D* ***8***
(off Teign St.)
Pellew Ho. *TQ14: Teignm 5D* ***8***
(off Teign St.)
Pellew Way TQ14: Teignm 2C **8**
Pembroke Pk. TQ3: Marl 6B **18**
Pembroke Rd. TQ1: Torq 4C **20**
TQ3: Paig 4B **22**
Pencorse Rd. TQ2: Torq 1A **20**
Pendennis Rd. TQ2: Torq 1A **20**
Penfield Gdns. EX7: Daw 4D **2**
Pengelly Way TQ2: Torq 4D **16**
Penn Ct. TQ5: Brixh 4E **29**
Pennine Dr. TQ4: Coll M 1A **24**
PENNINN 4A **12**
Penn Inn Cl. TQ12: New A 3B **12**
Penn La. TQ5: Brixh 4D **28**
Penn Mdws. TQ5: Brixh 4E **29**
Penn Mdws. Cl. TQ5: Brixh 4E **29**
Pennsylvania Rd. TQ1: Torq 4C **20**
Pennyacre Rd. TQ14: Teignm 3E **9**
Penny's Hill TQ1: Torq 2A **20**
Penpethy Cl. TQ5: Brixh 3C **28**
Penpethy Ct. TQ5: Brixh 3C **28**
Penpethy Rd. TQ5: Brixh 2C **28**
Penrhyn Pl. TQ14: Shal 6C **8**
Penshurst Rd. TQ12: New A 4G **11**
Pensilva Pk. TQ5: Brixh 4D **28**
Pentridge Av. TQ2: Torq 1F **23**
Penwill Way TQ4: Good, Paig . . .1C **24**
Peppermint Pk. Holiday Pk.
EX7: Daw W 1G **3**
Peppery La. TQ14: Shal 6B **8**
Peregrine Cl. TQ2: Torq 4C **16**
Perinville Cl. TQ1: Torq 3F **21**
Perinville Rd. TQ1: Torq 2E **21**
Perros Cl. TQ14: Teignm 3B **8**
Peters Cres. TQ3: Marl 6A **18**
Petitor M. TQ1: Torq 6G **17**
Petitor Rd. TQ1: Torq 6G **17**
Petitwell La. TQ1: Torq 6G **17**
Petrel Cl. TQ2: Torq 4B **16**
Petroc Dr. TQ12: New A 1H **11**
Phoenix Pl. TQ7: W Alv 4A **34**
Picket Head Hill TQ14: Shal 6C **8**
Pidgley Rd. EX7: Daw 1F **3**
Piermont Pl. EX7: Daw 4E **3**
Pillar Av. TQ5: Brixh 2C **28**
Pillar Cl. TQ5: Brixh 2C **28**
Pillar Cres. TQ5: Brixh 2C **28**
Pilmuir Av. TQ2: Torq 4H **19**
Pimlico TQ1: Torq 4C **20**
Pimm Rd. TQ3: Paig 4B **22**
Pine Cl. TQ5: Brixh 5C **28**
TQ14: Teignm 2F **9**
Pine Ct. TQ1: Torq 4E **21**
Pines Rd. TQ3: Paig 3B **22**
Pine Vw. Av. TQ1: Torq 3D **20**
Pine Vw. Gdns. TQ1: Torq 3D **20**
Pine Vw. Rd. TQ1: Torq 3D **20**
Pinewood Cl. EX7: Daw 2G **3**
Pinewood Rd. TQ12: New A 3B **12**
Pioneer Ter. TQ11: B'leigh 4A **32**
Pipehouse La. TQ13: Chud K 1H **5**
Pippins M. *TQ13: Ashb 3G* ***33***
(off Eastern Rd.)
Pitcairn Cres. TQ2: Torq 4D **16**
Pitland La. TQ12: Dacc 1D **16**
Pitley Rd. TQ13: Ashb 3H **33**
Pitt Hill Rd. TQ12: New A 6A **6**
Pitt La. EX7: Daw 3B **2**
Place La. TQ13: Ashb 2G **33**
PLAINMOOR 2C **20**
Plainmoor 2C **20**
Plainmoor Rd. TQ1: Torq 2C **20**
Plains, The TQ9: Tot 4G **31**
Plantation Cl. TQ12: New A 4C **12**
Plantation Ter. EX7: Daw 4D **2**
Plantation Way TQ2: Torq 5B **16**
Plant World of Devon 6F **13**
Platt Cl. TQ8: Salc 3E **35**
Platway La. TQ14: Shal 6B **8**
Pleasant Ter. TQ3: Paig 5D **22**
Plym Cl. TQ2: Torq 2E **19**
Plymouth Rd. TQ7: Kingsb 1A **34**
TQ9: Tot 4E **31**
TQ11: B'leigh, Lwr D 6A **32**
(not continuous)
TQ13: Chud K 1H **5**
Polhearne La. TQ5: Brixh 4C **28**
Polhearne Way TQ5: Brixh 4C **28**
Pollyblank Rd. TQ12: New A . . .2G **11**
Polsham Pk. TQ3: Paig 4E **23**
Pomeroy Av. TQ5: Brixh 2B **28**
Pomeroy Rd. TQ12: New A 2G **11**
Pomeroy Vs. TQ9: Tot 3G **31**
Pook La. TQ13: Ashb 3F **33**
Poplar Cl. TQ5: Brixh 6A **28**
TQ12: New A 5D **12**
Poplar Dr. TQ7: Kingsb 3B **34**
Poplars, The TQ13: Chud K 1H **5**
Poplars Dr. TQ3: Marl 1A **22**
Poplar Ter. TQ12: Ipp 5B **14**
Porlock Way TQ4: Paig 3C **24**
Portland Av. TQ14: Teignm 2E **9**
Portland Ct. *TQ1: Torq 2E* ***21***
(off Portland Rd.)
Portland Rd. TQ1: Torq 2E **21**
Potters Hill TQ1: Torq 4C **20**
Pottery, The *TQ6: Dartm 6D* ***30***
(off Warfleet Creek Rd.)
Pottery Cl. TQ13: Bov T 5B **4**
Pottery Cotts. *TQ6: Dartm 6D* ***30***
(off Warfleet Creek Rd.)
Pottery Ct. TQ6: Dartm 4A **30**
Pottery Rd. TQ12: Kingst 5E **7**
TQ13: Bov T 5B **4**
Pound Fld. TQ9: Sto G 5A **24**
Pound La. TQ12: Kingsk 3G **15**
TQ14: Shal 6A **8**
TQ14: Teignm 5E **9**
Pound Pl. *TQ12: New A 2G* ***11***
(off Jubilee Rd.)
TQ13: Bov T 2C **4**
Poundsgate Cl. TQ5: Brixh 3F **29**
Poundstone Ct. TQ8: Salc 3G **35**
Powderham Cl. TQ12: New A . . .3G **11**
Powderham Ct. *TQ12: New A . . .2G* ***11***
(off Powderham Rd.)
Powderham Rd. TQ2: Torq 6E **17**
TQ12: New A 2G **11**
Powderham Ter.
TQ12: New A 3G **11**
TQ14: Teignm 5E **9**
Precinct, The TQ7: Kingsb 2C **34**
PRESTON
TQ3 . . . . .2F **23**
TQ12 . . . . .1C **6**
Preston Down Av. TQ3: Pres 1E **23**
Preston Down Rd. TQ3: Pres . . .6B **18**
Prickly Ball Farm
(Hedgehog Hospital) 6E **11**
Prigg Mdw. TQ13: Ashb 4F **33**
Primley Ct. TQ3: Paig 6B **22**
PRIMLEY CROSS 6C **22**
Primley Pk. TQ3: Paig 6C **22**
Primley Pk. E. TQ3: Paig 6D **22**
Primrose Cl. TQ12: Kingst 4F **7**
Primrose Way TQ12: Kingsk 1G **15**
Prince Albert Pl. *EX7: Daw 4D* ***2***
(off Brook St.)
Prince Charles Ct. TQ2: Torq . . .4F **17**
Prince of Wales Dr.
TQ6: Dartm 3C **30**
Prince of Wales Rd.
TQ7: Kingsb 3B **34**
Prince Rupert Way
TQ12: Heat 4F **5**
Prince's Point TQ1: Torq 6D **20**
Princes Rd. TQ1: Torq 4C **20**
Princes Rd. E. TQ1: Torq 4D **20**
Princes Rd. W. TQ1: Torq 4C **20**
Princess Gdns. *6C* ***20***
(off Princess Pde.)
Princess Pde. TQ2: Torq 6C **20**
Princess Rd. TQ12: Kingsk 3H **15**
TQ12: Kingst 3E **7**
Princess Theatre 6B **20**

Princes St.—St Edmunds

Princes St. EX7: Daw 4D 2
TQ1: Torq 2E 21
TQ3: Paig 5E 23
Prince St. TQ12: New A 2H 11
Prince William Ct.
TQ5: Brixh 3D 28
Prings Ct. *TQ5: Brixh 2D 28*
(off Market St.)
Priory TQ13: Bov T 2B 4
Priory, The TQ12: A'well 6H 11
Priory Av. TQ9: Tot 3F 31
TQ12: Kingsk 2H 15
Priory Ct. TQ9: Tot 4F 31
Priory Dr. TQ9: Tot 3F 31
Priory Gdns. EX7: Daw 4E 3
TQ9: Tot 3F 31
Priory Ga. TQ9: Tot 3F 31
Priory Hill EX7: Daw 4E 3
TQ9: Tot 3F 31
Priory Pk. Rd. EX7: Daw 4D 2
Priory Rd. EX7: Daw 4E 3
TQ1: Torq 1C 20
TQ12: A'well 6G 11
Priory St. TQ6: Kingsw 5D 30
Priory Ter. *TQ9: Tot 3F 31*
(off Priory Hill)
Priscott Way TQ12: Kingst 5F 7
Promenade TQ3: Pres 3G 23
TQ4: Broads 6G 25
TQ4: Good 1F 25
(not continuous)
TQ7: Kingsb 3C 34
TQ14: Teignm 5E 9
Prospect Rd. TQ5: Brixh 2D 28
Prospect Steps *TQ5: Brixh 2D 28*
(off Sth. Furzeham Rd.)
Prospect Ter. TQ12: New A 2H 11
Puddavine Ter. TQ9: Darti 1E 31
Puffin Cl. TQ2: Torq 5B 16
Pump St. TQ5: Brixh 2E 29
Purbeck Av. TQ2: Torq 1F 23

Q

Quantocks Rd. TQ2: Torq 6F 19
Quarry Gdns. TQ3: Paig 4D 22
Quay, The TQ5: Brixh 2E 29
TQ6: Ditt 1B 30 (5A 26)
TQ7: Kingsb 3B 34
(off Prince of Wales Rd.)
TQ8: Bat 1F 35
Quay La. TQ7: Kingsb 3C 34
Quay Rd. TQ12: New A 2A 12
(not continuous)
TQ14: Teignm 5D 8
Quayside Leisure Cen. 4C 34
Quay Ter. TQ12: New A 2A 12
Quaywest Waterpark 2F 25
Queen Annes Copse
TQ12: E Ogw 4E 11
Queen Elizabeth Av.
TQ6: Dartm 3B 30
Queen Elizabeth Dr.
TQ3: Paig 5B 22
Queen La. EX7: Daw 4D 2
Queens Cl. TQ12: Kingst 3G 7
Queen's Cres. TQ5: Brixh 4E 29
Queen's Pk. Rd. TQ4: Paig 5F 23
Queen's Rd. TQ4: Paig 5F 23
TQ5: Brixh 1D 28
Queens Steps *TQ5: Brixh 2E 29*
(off King St.)
Queen's Ter. TQ9: Tot 3F 31
Queen St. EX7: Daw 4D 2
TQ1: Torq 4C 20
TQ12: New A 2H 11
TQ14: Teignm 5D 8
Queensway TQ2: Torq 3G 19
TQ12: New A 3B 12
Queensway Cl. TQ2: Torq 2H 19
Queensway Cres. TQ2: Torq 2H 19
Queensway Ho. TQ12: New A 3B 12
Quentin Av. TQ5: Brixh 5C 28
Quinnell Ho. *TQ14: Teignm 4C 8*
(off Coombe Va. Rd.)
Quinta Cl. TQ1: Torq 3D 20
Quinta Ct. TQ1: Torq 2D 20
Quinta Rd. TQ1: Torq 3D 20

R

Rack Pk. Rd. TQ7: Kingsb 3C 34
Raddicombe Dr. TQ5: Hill 6A 28
Radford Grange EX7: Daw 3A 2
Radnor Ter. TQ9: Tot 3F 31
Radway Gdns. TQ14: Bi'ton 5H 9
Radway Hill TQ14: Bi'ton 5H 9
Radway St. TQ14: Bi'ton 5H 9
Rainbow Ct. TQ2: Torq 2H 19
Raleigh Av. TQ2: Torq 3G 19
Raleigh Cl. TQ2: Torq 3G 19
TQ6: Dartm 4A 30
Raleigh Dr. TQ4: Good 3E 25
Raleigh Rd. TQ6: Dartm 3B 30
TQ8: Salc 3F 35
TQ12: New A 2C 12
TQ14: Teignm 2C 8
Raleigh St.
TQ6: Dartm 1B 30 (4C 30)
Ramparts Wlk. *TQ9: Tot 4F 31*
(off High St.)
Ramshill Rd. TQ3: Paig 3B 22
Randolph Ct. TQ12: New A 1F 11
Rangers Cl. TQ11: B'leigh 5B 32
Ranscombe Cl. TQ5: Brixh 2F 29
Ranscombe Rd. TQ5: Brixh 2E 29
Rathlin *TQ1: Torq 2D 20*
(off Palermo Rd.)
Rathmore Rd. TQ2: Torq 5H 19
(not continuous)
Ravensbury Dr. TQ6: Dartm 5D 30
Rawlyn Rd. TQ2: Torq 5G 19
Rea Barn Cl. TQ5: Brixh 3E 29
Rea Barn Rd. TQ5: Brixh 3E 29
Rea Dr. TQ5: Brixh 2E 29
Rear Dunmere Rd.
TQ1: Torq 3C 20
(off Dunmere Rd.)
Rectory Rd. TQ12: E Ogw 4D 10
Redavon Ri. TQ2: Torq 1E 19
Red Brook Cl. TQ4: Good 4F 25
Redburn Cl. TQ3: Paig 4D 22
Redburn Rd. TQ3: Paig 4D 22
Redcliffe Ct. TQ3: Pres 4G 23
Redcliffe Rd. TQ1: Torq 6H 17
Reddenhill Rd. TQ1: Torq 3D 20
Redford Mdw. TQ7: Kingsb 3B 34
Redford Way TQ7: Kingsb 3B 34
Redgate Cl. TQ1: Torq 3E 21
Red Ho. Cl. TQ13: Chud K 1H 5
Redlands Ct. TQ3: Paig 4C 22
REDLANDS INDEPENDENT HOSPITAL
3H 31
Redoubt Hill TQ6: Kingsw 4D 30
Redstart Cl. TQ12: E Ogw 4E 11
Redwalls Mdw. TQ6: Dartm 3B 30
Redwell La. TQ3: Paig 3C 22
Redwell Rd. TQ3: Paig 3C 22
Redwood Cl. TQ13: Bov T 6B 4
Redwood Ct. EX7: Daw 4E 3
Redwoods TQ13: Bov T 5B 4
Redworth Ct. *TQ9: Tot 3E 31*
(off Station Rd.)
Redworth Ter. TQ9: Tot 3F 31
Reed Va. TQ14: Teignm 4C 8
Reel Cinema, The
Kingsbridge 3B 34
Reeves Cl. *TQ9: Tot 4G 31*
(off New Wlk.)
Reeves Rd., The TQ2: Torq 4G 19
Regent Cl. TQ2: Torq 1H 19
Regent Gdns. *TQ14: Teignm 5E 9*
(off Regent St.)
Regents Ct. TQ4: Paig 6F 23
Regent St. EX7: Daw 4D 2
TQ14: Teignm 5E 9
Rendells Mdw. TQ13: Bov T 3D 4
Retreat Cl. TQ7: Kingsb 3B 34
REW 2F 33
Rewlea Cotts. TQ13: Ashb 2F 33
Rew Rd. TQ13: Ashb 1F 33
Reynell Av. TQ12: New A 2C 12
Reynell Rd. TQ12: E Ogw 5E 11
Rhine Vs. TQ9: Tot 4G 31
Rhodanthe Rd. TQ3: Pres 2E 23
Richards Cl. EX7: Daw 5D 2
Richardson Wlk. *TQ1: Torq 3A 20*
(off Barton Rd.)
Richmond Cl. TQ1: Torq 4H 21
Richmond Ct. *EX7: Daw 4E 3*
(off Richmond Pl.)
TQ3: Paig 4E 23
Richmond Hill
TQ12: Kingsk 2H 15
Richmond Pl. EX7: Daw 4E 3
Ridge Hill TQ6: Dartm 3C 30
Ridge La. TQ3: Marl 1C 18
Ridgemark Cl. TQ5: Brixh 2F 29
Ridge Rd. TQ1: Maid 1G 17
TQ12: Hacc, Neth 2G 13
TQ12: S'head 1G 17
Ridges, The TQ6: Dartm 5A 30
Ridgeway Cl. TQ12: New A 4C 12
Ridgeway Hgts. TQ1: Torq 5E 21
Ridgeway Hill TQ3: Comp 3A 18
Ridgeway La. TQ12: Coff 1B 16
Ridgeway Rd. TQ1: Torq 6E 21
TQ12: New A 4B 12
Ridley Hill TQ6: Kingsw 5D 30
Rillage La. TQ2: Torq 3A 20
RINGMORE 6B 8
Ringmore Cl. TQ14: Shal 6B 8
Ringmore Rd. TQ14: Shal 6A 8
Ringrone TQ8: Salc 5E 35
Ringslade Cl. TQ12: New A 6A 6
Ringslade Rd. TQ12: New A 5A 6
Rippon Cl. TQ5: Brixh 5A 28
River Cl. TQ12: Kingst 6G 7
Riverside TQ9: Tot 2E 31
TQ14: Shal 6C 8
Riverside 2 TQ12: New A 1A 12
Riverside Ct. *TQ6: Dartm 1B 30*
(off South Embankment)
TQ12: New A 1A 12
Riverside Mill
(The Devon Guild of Craftsmen)
3C 4
Riverside Rd. TQ6: Ditt 4A 26
Riverview TQ12: New A 3C 12
Riverview Pl. *TQ7: Kingsb 3B 34*
(off Fore St.)
Riviera, The *TQ1: Torq 6C 20*
(off Parkhill Rd.)
TQ4: Paig 6E 23
Riviera Ct. TQ1: Torq 5D 20
Riviera International Cen. 5A 20
Riviera Ter. EX7: Daw 3F 3
Riviera Way TQ2: Torq 6A 16
Robers Rd. TQ12: Kingst 3E 7
Roberts Cl. TQ2: Torq 5G 17
Roberts Way TQ12: New A 1E 11
Robinsons Row *TQ8: Salc 3H 35*
(off Fore St.)
Roborough Gdns. TQ13: Ashb 2G 33
Roborough La. TQ13: Ashb 3F 33
Roborough Ter. TQ13: Ashb 3F 33
Rock Cl. TQ4: Broads 6F 25
Rock End Av. TQ1: Torq 6D 20
Rockfield Cl. TQ14: Teignm 2F 9
Rock Ho. La. TQ1: Maid 3H 17
Rock Pk. TQ6: Dartm 3A 30
TQ13: Ashb 2G 33
Rock Rd. TQ2: Torq 5C 20
Rockstone, The EX7: Daw 3G 3
Rock Wlk. TQ2: Torq 5B 20
Rocky La. TQ11: B'leigh 6A 32
TQ14: Teignm 3C 8
(not continuous)
Rocombe Cl. TQ2: Torq 3E 17
Rocombe Hill TQ12: Coff 6H 13
Rodgers Ind. Est. TQ4: Paig 2A 24
Rodney Cl. TQ6: Dartm 4A 30
Rogada Ct. TQ5: Brixh 5E 29
Romaleyn Gdns. TQ4: Good 1E 25
Rookery Cotts. TQ3: Marl 5A 18
Rooklands Av. TQ1: Torq 2A 20
Rope Wlk. TQ14: Teignm 4D 8
Ropewalk TQ7: Kingsb 4B 34
Ropewalk Hill TQ5: Brixh 2D 28
Rose Acre Ter. TQ5: Brixh 3E 29
Rose Dene TQ2: Torq 5E 17
Rose Gdns. TQ12: Ipp 5C 14
Rose Hill TQ12: Kingsk 3G 15
Rose Hill Cl. TQ12: Kingsk 3G 15
Rosehill Cl. TQ1: Torq 4D 20
Rosehill Gdns. TQ12: Kingsk 3G 15
Rosehill Rd. TQ1: Torq 4C 20
Roselands Dr. TQ4: Paig 2B 24
Roseland Sq. TQ12: Kingst 4F 7
Roselands Rd.
TQ4: Good, Paig 2C 24
TQ4: Paig 2B 24
Rosemary Av. TQ12: New A 1E 11
Rosemary Ct. TQ3: Pres 3E 23
Rosemary Gdns. TQ3: Paig 3C 22
Rosemont TQ1: Torq 5E 21
Rosemount *TQ4: Good 1F 25*
(off Roundham Rd.)
Rosemount Ct. *TQ8: Salc 2G 35*
(off Church St.)
Rosery Rd. TQ2: Torq 4H 19
Roseville St.
TQ6: Dartm 1A 30 (4C 30)
Rosewarne Av. TQ12: New A 3C 12
Rossall Dr. TQ3: Paig 6D 22
Ross Pk. Caravan Pk.
TQ12: Ipp 4A 14
Rosyl Av. EX7: Holc 1G 9
Rotherfold TQ9: Tot 4E 31
Rougemont Av. TQ2: Torq 6B 16
Round Berry Dr. TQ8: Salc 3F 35
Roundham Av. TQ4: Good 1G 25
Roundham Cres. TQ4: Good 6G 23
Roundham Gdns. TQ4: Good 1F 25
Roundham Ho. *TQ4: Paig 6F 23*
(off Belle Vue Rd.)
Roundham Rd. TQ4: Paig 6F 23
Roundhead Rd. TQ12: Heat 3E 5
ROUND HILL 1F 23
Roundhill Rd. TQ2: Torq 1G 23
Roundings, The TQ5: Galm 2E 27
Roundmoors Cl.
TQ12: Kingsk 4H 15
Roundway, The
TQ12: Kingsk 1G 15
Rousdown Rd. TQ2: Torq 5H 19
Rowan Cl. TQ12: E Ogw 4E 11
Rowantree Rd. TQ12: New A 4B 12
Rowan Way TQ5: Brixh 5A 28
Rowbrook Cl. TQ4: Paig 2B 24
ROWCROFT HOSPICE 3H 19
Rowcroft Rd. TQ3: Pres 3F 23
Rowdens, The *TQ2: Torq 4A 20*
(off Belgrave Rd.)
TQ14: Teignm 3F 9
Rowdens Rd. TQ2: Torq 4A 20
Rowes Farm Barns
TQ9: Sto G 5A 24
Rowley Rd. TQ1: Torq 1D 20
Rowsell's La. TQ9: Tot 4G 31
Royal Ct. *TQ1: Torq 2E 21*
(off Bedford Rd.)
TQ12: New A 2H 11
TQ14: Teignm 5E 9
(off Den Cres.)
Royal Dart Yacht Club 5D 30
Royal Pines TQ1: Torq 6E 21
Royal Terrace Gdns. 5B 20
Royal Torbay Yacht Club 6C 20
Rozel TQ1: Torq 6E 21
Ruckamore Rd. TQ2: Torq 4H 19
Rundle Rd. TQ12: New A 1H 11
Rushlade Cl. TQ4: Paig 3C 24
Rush Way TQ9: Tot 4H 31
Russell Ct. *TQ8: Salc 2H 35*
(off Fore St.)
TQ9: Tot 4F 31
Russets La. TQ11: B'leigh 4C 32
Ryde Cl. TQ2: Torq 5F 17
Ryders Bank TQ11: B'leigh 5A 32
RYDON 3F 7
Rydon Acres TQ9: Sto G 5A 24
TQ12: Kingst 3F 7
Rydon Av. TQ12: Kingst 3F 7
Rydon Est. TQ12: Kingst 3F 7
Rydon Ind. Est. TQ12: Kingst 5E 7
Rydon La. TQ12: A'well 1D 14
Rydon Path TQ12: Kingst 2F 7
Rydon Rd. TQ12: Kingst 2F 7
Rydons TQ5: Brixh 3B 28

S

Sackery TQ12: C'head 1G 13
Saddle, The TQ4: Good 3F 25
Saffron Ct. TQ7: Kingsb 3C 34
Saffron Pk. TQ7: Kingsb 3C 34
St Agnes La. TQ2: Torq 6H 19
St Albans La. TQ1: Torq 2D 20
St Albans Rd. TQ1: Torq 2D 20
St Andrews Cl. TQ13: Ashb 4F 33
St Andrews Rd. TQ4: Paig 6F 23
St Anne's Ct. TQ12: New A 2F 11
St Anne's Rd. TQ1: Torq 2D 20
St Augustine's Cl. TQ2: Torq 4F 17
St Bartholomew Way
TQ12: E Ogw 5C 10
St Bernard's Cl. TQ11: Buck 2B 32
(not continuous)
St Catherine's Rd. TQ1: Torq 1C 20
St Clements Ct. *TQ6: Dartm 3B 30*
(off Church Rd.)
St Columba Cl. TQ12: Kingst 3F 7
St Davids Rd. TQ14: Teignm 1D 8
St Dominics Cl. TQ1: Torq 1C 20
St Dunstans Rd. TQ8: Salc 3F 35
St Edmunds TQ7: Kingsb 2B 34

48 A-Z Torbay

St Edmund's Rd.—Southern Cl.

St Edmund's Rd. TQ1: Torq 2C 20
(not continuous)
St Edmunds Wlk.
TQ7: Kingsb 3B 34
St Efride's Rd. TQ2: Torq 4A 20
St Elmo Ct. TQ8: Salc 4E 35
St George's Ct. TQ2: Torq 4G 17
St Georges Cres. TQ1: Torq 2D 20
St George's Rd. TQ1: Torq 2D 20
St Georges Sq. *TQ6: Dartm 2B 30*
(off Newcomen Rd.)
St Ive's Ct. TQ1: Torq 3B 20
St James Pl. TQ1: Torq 2E 21
St James Rd. TQ1: Torq 2B 20
St James's Ho. *TQ14: Teignm . . .4D 8*
(off Fore St.)
St James's Pct. *TQ14: Teignm . . .4D 8*
(off Bitton Pk. Rd.)
St John's Cl. TQ13: Bov T 4B 4
TQ14: Bi'ton 6G 9
St John's Ct. *TQ3: Paig 5E 23*
(off Littlegate Rd.)
TQ9: Tot 4G 31
(off Weston Rd.)
St Johns La. TQ13: Bov T 3B 4
St Johns Pl. *TQ1: Torq 5C 20*
(off Braddons Hill Rd. W.)
St Johns St. TQ12: New A 1H 11
St John's Ter. TQ9: Tot 3E 31
St Josephs Ct. *TQ14: Teignm 5E 9*
(off Carlton Pl.)
St Katherine's M. *TQ9: Tot 4F 31*
(off St Katherine's Way)
St Katherine's Rd. TQ1: Torq . . .3H 19
St Katherine's Way TQ9: Tot 4F 31
St Kitts Cl. TQ2: Torq 5E 17
St Lawrence La. TQ13: Ashb . . .4F 33
St Leonard's Cl.
TQ12: New A 3G 11
St Leonard's Rd.
TQ12: New A 3G 11
St Leonard's Tower 2G 11
St Luke's Cl. TQ12: New A 4C 12
St Lukes Dr. TQ14: Teignm 3C 8
St Luke's Pk. TQ2: Torq 5B 20
St Luke's Rd. TQ2: Torq 4B 20
TQ12: New A 4B 12
St Luke's Rd. Nth. TQ2: Torq . . .5B 20
St Luke's Rd. Sth. TQ2: Torq . . .5B 20
St Marco Gdns. TQ7: Kingsb . . .2C 34
St Margaret's Av. TQ1: Torq 2C 20
St Margaret's Cl. TQ1: Torq 1C 20
St Margaret's M. TQ1: Torq 1C 20
St Margaret's Rd. TQ1: Torq 1C 20
St Mark's Dr. *TQ1: Torq 6E 21*
(off St Mark's Rd.)
St Mark's Rd. TQ1: Torq 6E 21
St Martins Ct. TQ2: Torq 6E 17
St Martin's M. *TQ1: Torq 1D 20*
(off Fore St.)
ST MARYCHURCH 6H 17
St Marychurch Rd. TQ1: Torq . . .6G 17
(not continuous)
TQ12: Coff, Dacc, New A, S'head
. . . . .3B 12
St Mary Magdalen Cl.
TQ14: Bi'ton 6G 9
St Mary's Bay Holiday Cen.
TQ5: Brixh 4F 29
St Marys Cl. TQ5: Brixh 5C 28
TQ12: A'well 1B 14
St Marys Ct. TQ3: Paig 5D 22
TQ12: New A 2G 11
(off Highweek St.)
St Mary's Dr. TQ5: Brixh 4E 29
St Mary's Hill TQ5: Brixh 4E 29
St Mary's Pk. TQ4: Coll M 1A 24
St Mary's Rd. TQ5: Brixh 5D 28
TQ12: New A 3G 11
TQ14: Teignm 2C 8
St Mary's Sq. TQ5: Brixh 4C 28
St Matthew's Rd. TQ2: Torq 5G 19
St Matthias Chu. Rd.
TQ1: Torq 4F 21
St Mawes Dr. TQ4: Good 5E 25
ST MICHAEL'S 6E 23
St Michael's Cl. TQ1: Torq 3H 19
St Michael's Ct. *TQ4: Paig 1D 24*
(off Derrell Rd.)
St Michael's Rd. TQ1: Torq 2H 19
TQ4: Paig 6D 22
TQ12: Kingst 5E 7
TQ12: New A 4A 12
TQ14: Teignm 2E 9
St Michael's Ter. TQ1: Torq 4C 20
St Pails Ct. *TQ1: Torq 2C 20*
(off St Edmunds Rd.)
St Patricks Cl. TQ14: Teignm 3C 8
St Pauls Cl. TQ13: Bov T 3C 4
St Paul's Cres. TQ1: Torq 2C 20
St Paul's Rd. TQ1: Torq 2C 20
TQ3: Pres 2G 23
TQ12: New A 2H 11
St Peters Cl. TQ2: Torq 3G 19
TQ13: Bov T 2D 4
St Peter's Hill TQ5: Brixh 2E 29
St Peter's Quay TQ9: Tot 5G 31
St Peters Ter. *TQ5: Brixh 2E 29*
(off Elkins Hill)
St Scholasticas TQ14: Teignm . . .2F 9
St Thomas Cl. TQ13: Bov T 3D 4
St Vincent's Cl. TQ1: Torq 3A 20
St Vincent's Rd. TQ1: Torq 2A 20
SALCOMBE 2H 35
Salcombe (Park & Ride) 2F 35
Salcombe Hgts. Cl.
TQ8: Salc 2F 35
Salcombe Maritime &
Local History Mus. 2H 35
Salcombe RNLI Mus. 2H 35
Salcombe Rd. TQ7: Malb 1E 35
Salcombe Yacht Club 3G 35
Salem Pl. TQ12: New A 2G 11
Salisbury Av. TQ2: Torq 5E 17
Salisbury Rd. TQ12: New A 1A 12
Salisbury Ter. TQ14: Teignm 4E 9
Salmon Leap Cl.
TQ11: B'leigh 4C 32
Saltern Rd. TQ4: Good 4F 25
Saltings, The TQ14: Shal 6B 8
Salt Quay Moorings
TQ7: Kingsb 4C 34
(off Embankment Rd.)
Salty La. TQ14: Shal 6B 8
Samara Bus. Pk. TQ12: Heat 3E 5
Sanders Rd. TQ5: Brixh 2B 28
Sandford Orleigh
TQ12: New A 6C 6
Sandford Vw. TQ12: New A 1G 11
Sandhills Rd. TQ8: Salc 4F 35
Sand Martins, The
TQ12: New A 3B 12
(off St Marychurch Rd.)
Sandown Rd. TQ4: Paig 3C 24
Sandpath Rd. TQ12: Kingst 5F 7
Sandpiper Way TQ2: Torq 5B 16
Sandquay Rd. TQ6: Dartm 2C 30
Sandringham Dr. TQ3: Pres 1D 22
Sandringham Gdns.
TQ3: Pres 1E 23
Sandringham Rd.
TQ12: New A 2B 12
Sands Beach Wlk. TQ4: Good . . .3F 25
Sands Ct. TQ4: Paig 6E 23
Sands Rd. TQ4: Paig 6E 23
SANDYGATE 2E 7
Sandygate TQ12: Kingst 2D 6
Sandygate Bus. Pk.
TQ12: Kingst 2D 6
Sandygate M. *TQ12: Kingst 1E 7*
(off Lower Sandygate)
Sandygate Mill TQ12: Kingst 1E 7
Sandy La. EX7: Daw 2F 3
Sanford Rd. TQ2: Torq 4H 19
San Remo Ter. EX7: Daw 4F 3
Saturday's La. TQ12: N Whil . . .6G 15
Sawyer Dr. TQ14: Teignm 2B 8
Saxon Hgts. TQ5: Brixh 3D 28
Saxon Mdw. TQ4: Coll M 6A 22
Scarborough Pl. TQ2: Torq 4A 20
Scarborough Rd. TQ2: Torq 4A 20
Scholars Wlk. TQ7: Kingsb 2C 34
School Cotts. TQ12: Teigng 3B 6
School Ct. TQ6: Dartm 4A 30
School Hill EX7: Daw 4D 2
TQ9: Sto G 6A 24
School Hill Cotts. *TQ9: Sto G . . .6A 24*
(off School Hill)
School La. TQ14: Shal 6C 8
School Rd. TQ12: Kingsk 2G 15
TQ12: New A 2H 11
TQ12: Teigng 3A 6
School Steps TQ6: Dartm 2A 30
School Ter. *EX7: Daw 4D 2*
(off School Hill)
Scoresby Cl. TQ2: Torq 3G 17
Scott Cinemas
The Alexandra Cinema . . .2G 11
Scratton Path *TQ12: E Ogw 5E 11*
(off Reynell Rd.)
Screechers Hill TQ13: Ashb 3E 33
Seabourne Ct. *TQ4: Good 1F 25*
(off Alta Vista Rd.)
Seacliff TQ14: Teignm 3F 9
Seafields TQ4: Good 3F 25
Sea Front TQ2: Torq 1H 23
Sea La. TQ5: Brixh 3F 29
Sea Lawn Ter. EX7: Daw 3F 3
Seale Cl. TQ6: Dartm 3A 30
Seapoint *TQ14: Teignm 5D 8*
(off Strand)
Seascape TQ2: Torq 6A 20
Seashore Centre, The 1F 25
Seaton Cl. TQ1: Torq 2E 21
Seaview Cres. TQ3: Pres 2F 23
Sea Vw. Ter. *TQ5: Brixh 1D 28*
(off Overgang Rd.)
Seaway Cl. TQ2: Torq 6H 19
Seaway Ct. TQ2: Torq 6A 20
TQ5: Brixh 3C 28
Seaway Cres. TQ3: Pres 3G 23
Seaway Gdns. TQ3: Pres 3G 23
Seaway La. TQ2: Torq 5G 19
Seaway Rd. TQ3: Pres 3F 23
Secmaton La. EX7: Daw 2E 3
Secmaton Ri. EX7: Daw 1E 3
Second Av. EX7: Daw 5C 2
TQ1: Torq 1B 20
TQ14: Teignm 4C 8
Second Dr. TQ14: Teignm 3F 9
(Burwood Pl.)
TQ14: Teignm 4D 8
(Third Dr.)
Sefton Ct. EX7: Daw 4D 2
TQ1: Torq 2E 21
Sellick Av. TQ5: Brixh 4E 29
Sett Cl. TQ13: Bov T 3C 4
Seven Hills Ho. *TQ2: Torq 4B 20*
(off Burridge La.)
Severn Rd. TQ2: Torq 2E 19
Seymour Dr. TQ2: Torq 3F 17
TQ6: Dartm 4A 30
(off Townstal Rd.)
Seymour Pl. TQ9: Tot 4G 31
Seymour Rd. TQ9: Tot 4G 31
TQ12: New A 1G 11
Shackleton Wlk.
TQ14: Teignm 1C 8
SHADYCOMBE 2G 35
Shadycombe Ct. TQ8: Salc 2G 35
Shadycombe Rd. TQ8: Salc 1F 35
Shady Nook Caravan Site
TQ12: Kingst 4F 7
Shaftesbury Cl. *EX7: Daw 4E 3*
(off Brunswick Pl.)
Shaftesbury Pl. *TQ9: Tot 4F 31*
(off Maudlin Rd.)
Shaftesbury Theatre
Dawlish 4D 2
Shakespeare Cl. TQ2: Torq 3G 19
SHALDON 6C 8
Shaldon Bri. TQ14: Shal 5C 8
Shaldon Rd. TQ12: C'head 1H 13
TQ12: New A 3B 12
TQ14: Shal 6A 8
(not continuous)
Shaldon Wildlife Trust 6D 8
Shapley Tor Cl. TQ5: Brixh 5B 28
Shaptor Vw. TQ13: Bov T 5A 4
Sharkham Ct. TQ5: Brixh 4E 29
Sharkham Dr. TQ5: Brixh 4E 29
Sharkham Ho. TQ5: Brixh 4E 29
Sharkham Point Caravan Pk.
TQ5: Brixh 5E 29
Sharpham Dr. TQ9: Tot 5G 31
Sharpitor TQ8: Salc 6E 35
Sharpitor Cl. TQ3: Pres 2C 22
Sharp's Cl. TQ12: Heat 4F 5
Sharp's Crest TQ12: Heat 4F 5
Shearwater Dr. TQ2: Torq 4C 16
Shedden Hill TQ2: Torq 5B 20
Shelley Av. TQ1: Torq 1B 20
Shelston Tor Dr. TQ4: Paig 2C 24
Shepherd Cl. TQ3: Paig 6B 22
Shepherd's La. TQ14: Teignm 1A 8
Sherborne Rd. TQ12: New A . . .2G 11
Sherwell Hill TQ2: Torq 4G 19
Sherwell La. TQ2: Torq 4G 19
Sherwell Pk. Rd. TQ2: Torq 4G 19
Sherwell Ri. Sth. TQ2: Torq 4G 19
Sherwell Valley Rd.
TQ2: Torq 3F 19
Shetland Cl. TQ2: Torq 5D 16
Shillingate Cl. EX7: Daw 6C 2
SHIPHAY 2F 19
Shiphay Av. TQ2: Torq 2F 19
Shiphay La. TQ2: Torq 1F 19
Shiphay Mnr. Dr. TQ2: Torq 2G 19
Shiphay Pk. Rd. TQ2: Torq 2G 19
Shirburn Rd. TQ1: Torq 2B 20
Shire Cl. TQ4: Good 5D 24
Shirley Ct. *TQ1: Torq 5E 21*
(off Torwood Gdns. Rd.)
Shirley Towers TQ1: Torq 6C 20
Shoalstone Pool 1F 29
Shobbrook Hill TQ12: New A . . .1D 10
Shoreside TQ14: Shal 6C 8
Shorland Cl. EX7: Daw 2F 3
SHORTON 2D 22
Shorton Rd. TQ3: Paig, Pres 3D 22
TQ3: Pres 2D 22
Shorton Valley Rd. TQ3: Pres . . .2D 22
Shrewsbury Av. TQ2: Torq 6F 17
Shute Ct. TQ14: Bi'ton 5H 9
Shute Hill TQ14: Bi'ton 5H 9
TQ14: Teignm 4E 9
Shute Hill Cres. TQ14: Teignm . . .4E 9
Shute Rd. TQ9: Tot 4G 31
Sidney Ct. *EX7: Daw 4D 2*
(off Old Town St.)
Sidney Wlk. TQ4: Good 4E 25
Silver Bri. Cl. TQ4: Good 5F 25
Silverhills Rd. TQ12: New A 5A 12
Silver St. TQ11: B'leigh 4B 32
TQ12: Ipp 6A 14
Silverwood Av. TQ12: New A . . .4B 12
Singer Cl. TQ3: Paig 6D 22
Singmore Rd. TQ3: Marl 1B 22
Skelmersdale Cl.
TQ7: Kingsb 3C 34
Skye Cl. TQ2: Torq 5D 16
Slade La. TQ5: Galm 2E 27
TQ12: A'well 1B 14
(not continuous)
Sladnor Pk. Rd. TQ1: Maid 2G 17
Slanns Mdw. TQ12: Kingst 5E 7
Sleepy La. TQ3: Pres 2D 22
Smallcombe Rd. TQ3: Paig 3B 22
Smalldon La. TQ1: Torq 4G 17
Smallwell La. TQ3: Marl 6A 18
Smardon Av. TQ5: Brixh 2B 28
Smardon Cl. TQ5: Brixh 2B 28
Smith Ct. TQ1: Torq 3A 20
Smithfields *TQ9: Tot 4E 31*
(off Plymouth Rd.)
Smith Hill TQ14: Bi'ton 5G 9
Smith St. TQ6: Dartm . . .1B 30 (4C 30)
Smokey Ho. Caravans
TQ3: Marl 1B 22
Smugglers Caravan Pk.
EX7: Holc 1G 9
Smugglers La. EX7: Holc 1H 9
Snowberry Cl. TQ1: Torq 2A 20
Snowdonia Cl. TQ4: Coll M 1A 24
Solsbro M. TQ2: Torq 5H 19
Solsbro Rd. TQ2: Torq 5H 19
Somerset Ct. *TQ5: Brixh 2E 29*
(off Mt. Pleasant Rd.)
Somerset Pl. TQ9: Tot 4G 31
TQ14: Teignm 5D 8
Soper Rd. TQ14: Teignm 2C 8
Soper Wlk. TQ14: Teignm 2C 8
Sophia Way TQ12: New A 3F 11
Sorrell Ct. TQ12: Kingst 4E 7
Sorrento TQ1: Torq 4D 20
Sth. Bay Holiday Camp
TQ5: Brixh 5E 29
SOUTHBROOK 1A 4
Southbrook Cl. TQ13: Bov T 2B 4
Southbrook La. TQ13: Bov T 2A 4
(not continuous)
Southbrook Rd. TQ13: Bov T 2B 4
Southcote Orchard TQ9: Tot 4H 31
Sth. Devon Coast Path
TQ14: Shal 6D 8
Sth. Devon M. TQ12: New A 2A 12
South Devon Railway
Buckfastleigh Station 4D 32
Totnes
(Littlehempston Riverside) Station
. . . . .2F 31
South Devon Railway Mus. 4D 32
Southdown Av. TQ5: Brixh 5C 28
Southdown Cl. TQ5: Brixh 5C 28
Southdown Hill TQ5: Brixh 5C 28
Southdown Rd. TQ5: Brixh 6C 28
Southdowns Rd. EX7: Daw 6D 2
South Embankment
TQ6: Dartm 2B 30 (4C 30)
Southern Cl. TQ2: Torq 3F 17

GUIDE TO SELECTED PLACES OF INTEREST

HOW TO USE THE GUIDE

Opening times for places of interest vary considerably depending on the season, day of the week or the ownership of the property. Please check opening times before starting your journey.

The index reference is to the square in which the place of interest appears. e.g. **Paignton Zoo** 1C **24**, is to be found in square 1C on page 24.

TORBAY

Torbay has three towns, Torquay, Paignton and Brixham, each with its own character and style. The area is also know as "The English Riviera", which, along with other seaside resorts, surrounding market towns and nearby Dartmoor, offer something of interest for everyone.

For holiday information - what to see, transport and accommodation there are Tourist Information Centres in a number of Torbay and South Devon towns.

© Jennifer Thompson. Image from BigStockPhoto.com

Torquay Harbour

Tourist Information Centre

Ashburton, **Town Hall, North Street TQ13 7QQ.**
Tel: 01364 653426. www.ashburton.org   4E **33**

Bovey Tracey, **Lower Car Park, Station Road,**
TQ13 9AW. Tel: 01626 832047.
www.boveytracey.gov.uk   3B **4**

Brixham, (Open Easter- October)
19-20 The Quay TQ5 8AW. Tel: 0844 474 2233.
www.englishriviera.co.uk   2E **29**

Buckfastleigh, **80 Fore Street TQ11 0BS.**
Tel: 01364 644522.   4C **32**

Dartmouth, **The Engine House, Mayors Avenue,**
TQ6 9YY. Tel: 01803 834224.
www.discoverdartmouth.com   1B **30**

Dawlish, **The Lawn EX7 9PW.**
Tel: 01626 215665.   4E **3**

Kingsbridge, **The Quay TQ7 1HS.**
Tel: 01548 853195.   3C **34**

Newton Abbot, **6 Bridge House, Courtenay Street,**
TQ12 2QS. Tel: 01626 215667.   2G **11**

Paignton, (Open Easter - October)
Esplanade Road, TQ4 6ED. Tel: 0844 474 2233.
www.englishriviera.co.uk   5F **23**

Salcombe, **Market Street TQ8 8DE.**
Tel: 01548 843927.   2H **35**

Shaldon, **Shaldon Car Park, Ness Drive TQ14 0HP.**
Tel: 01626 873723.   6D **8**

Teignmouth, **The Den, Sea Front TQ14 8BE.**
Tel: 01626 215666.   5E **9**

Torquay, **5 Vaughan Parade TQ2 5JG.**
Tel: 0844 474 2233.
www.englishriviera.co.uk   6C **20**

Totnes, **Town Mill, Coronation Road TQ9 5DF.**
Tel: 01803 863168.
www.totnesinformation.co.uk   4G **31**

scan this QR code for:
www.englishriviera.co.uk

Dartmouth River Boats
5 Lower Street TQ6 9AJ.
Tel: 01803 555872.
www.dartmouthrailriver.co.uk
Boat trips in Dartmouth Harbour, along the River Dart to Totnes and sea cruises to Salcombe and Torquay. (some trips are weather and sea conditions dependent).

Greenway Ferry and Pleasure Cruises
Princess Pier, Torbay Road, Torquay TQ2 5HA.
Tel: 01803 882811.
www.greenwayferry.co.uk
Boat trips from Torquay to Babbacombe, Brixham, Dartmouth and Greenway, also sightseeing and Sea-Fari wildlife cruises. Ferries from Dartmouth and Totnes to Greenway (Agatha Christie's House).

© Kevin Penhallow, image from BigStockPhoto.com

Paignton Pleasure Cruises
Roundham Road TQ4 6DW.
Tel: 01803 529147.
www.paigntonpleasurecruises.co.uk
Boat trips from Paignton, Torquay and Brixham

Rivermaid Kingsbridge-Salcombe Ferry
Embankment Road, Kingsbridge TQ7 1JZ.
Tel: 01803 834488.
www.kingsbridgesalcombeferry.co.uk
Summer ferry from Salcombe to Kingsbridge and also wildlife cruises in Salcombe Harbour.

Riviera Cruises
8 Ivy Lane TQ14 8BT.
Tel: 01626 774868.
www.rivieracruises.webs.com
Boat trips from Teignmouth on River Teign and around bay.

Torbay Belle Cruises (Brixham Belle Cruises)
Ocean View, 6 The Saddle, Paignton TQ4 6NQ.
Tel: 01803 528555.
Boat trips from Torquay and Brixham to Dartmouth, also sightseeing cruises.

Western Lady Ferry Service
Dolphin Shipyard, Galmpton, Brixham TQ5 0EH.
Tel: 01803 293797.
www.westernladyferry.com
Ferry from Torquay to Brixham

Ashburton Museum   4F 33
The Bull Ring, 1 West Street TQ13 7DT.
Tel: 01364 652698.
www.ashburton.org/museum.htm
An interesting local history collection explaining the importance of former wool processing and mining industries, together with displays on agriculture and Dartmoor. Here also is the Endacott Collection of North American Indian artifacts.
Limited opening in summer only.

Babbacombe Model Village   6H 17
Hampton Avenue TQ1 3LA.
Tel: 01803 315315.
www.babbacombemodelvillage.co.uk
Continously developed since 1963, the four acres of garden display an imaginary English countryside including both Town and Village settings complete with houses, shops, factories, railways, farms, country houses, lakes, waterfalls and thousands of

miniature people. Some well known landmarks are included together with 21st century updates including a wind farm and hydro electric dam. Sound and animation add to the spectacle.
The Village is also famous for its miniature landscaped gardens, including hundreds of plant varieties. There are various indoor exhibitions including a 4D Theatre and Model Railway. Evening illuminations can be seen at various times throughout the year.

Bayard's Cove Fort   5C 30
Dartmouth TQ6 9AT.
www.english-heritage.org.uk
This 16th century artillery fort, now in the care of English Heritage, stands guard over the narrowest point of the entrance to Dartmouth harbour. It was built as a last line of defence should enemy ships succeed in passing the defensive positions at the mouth of the estuary - Kingswear and Dartmouth Castles.

Berry Head

2H 29

Brixham TQ5 9AW.
A dramatic limestone headland and viewpoint with 60m sheer cliffs and open terrain. Berry Head Country Park contains the 100 acre Berry Head National Nature Reserve with its important rare plant and animal species. There are two well-preserved Napoleonic War Forts and a lighthouse, which at 5m tall is the shortest in Great Britain. The wildlife, geology and history of Berry Head are explored through interpretation displays in the visitor centre, a restored former guardhouse of 1804. The long distance South West Coast Path traverses the headland.

Bishopsteignton Museum of Rural Life

5H 9

Shute Hill TQ14 9QL.
Tel: 01626 775308.
www.teignbridge.gov.uk
Displays illustrate life and work in a small rural community together with items of local militaria, transportation and geology.
Limited opening in Summer only.

Brixham Heritage Museum

2D 28

The Old Police Station,
New Road TQ5 8LZ.
Tel: 01803 856267.
www.brixhamheritage.org.uk
Tells the story of this historic town, its people and the importance of the fishing industry. Room settings help to illustrate social history together with displays of costume and local memorabilia. Local archaeology and military history, including that of the the coastal Napoleonic forts, are also featured.

Buckfast Abbey

2C 32

Buckfastleigh TQ11 0EE.
Tel: 01364 645500.
www.buckfast.org.uk
The historic abbey founded in 1018 acquired great wealth trading in wool throughout the Middle Ages. Following the Dissolution of the Monasteries the abbey fell largely into ruin. In 1882 French monks refounded a small community rebuilding on the medieval foundations, though work on the Abbey church did not begin until 1907. Its construction by small groups of monks took 30 years to complete using a mixture of both English and French gothic style. Todays Roman Catholic Community of Benedictine monks are self-supporting producing pottery, stained glass, carving, Buckfast Tonic Wine and famously, honey from their own disease resistant Buckfast bee population.

Buckfast Butterflies & Dartmoor Otter Sanctuary

4D 32

The Station, Dart Brdge Road,
Buckfastleigh TQ11 0DZ.
Tel: 01364 642916.
www.ottersandbutterflies.co.uk
Both an attractive visitor destination and an educational experience. Within the Butterfly House, a tropical environment, exotic plants and flowers allow the observation of the complete life-cycle of the butterfly. See the spectacular colours and forms of these tropical creatures at close quarters. Learn about the secretive life and habits of the British Otter and watch them swim under water in a special observation pool. The Dartmoor Otter Sanctuary functions as a rescue centre and is designed to give its resident otters the best habitat possible.

Bygones

1D 20

Fore Street, St Marychurch, Torquay TQ1 4PR.
Tel: 01803 326108.
www.bygones.co.uk
Evocative displays of past-times within period re-creations include the Victorian shopping street, with its fully furnished and stocked general store, apothecary and toy shop. Victorian room displays include the nursery, kitchen and public house. Other features include a shopping arcade of the 1940's and 1950's and a World War I trench and militaria display.

© Andrew Gaylor, image from BigStockPhoto.com

Buckfast Abbey

Cockington Country Park   5F 19

Cockington Court, Cockington TQ2 6XA.
Tel: 01803 606035.
www.cockingtoncourt.org
The 460 acres of parkland surround the historic Court with its art galleries and Stable Yard craft centre workshops. As well as the open parkland, a demonstration organic garden and formal rose garden can be enjoyed. Elsewhere are lakes, watermeadows, woodland, farmland and orchards. There is a network of walking and cycling paths and a play area for children. The thatched village of Cockington, with its famous and much photographed ancient forge, is often quoted as one of England's prettiest villages.

© Jeff Gynane, image from BigStockPhoto.com

English cottage in Cockington

Compton Castle   3A 18

Marldon, Paignton TQ3 1TA.
Tel: 01803 661906.
www.nationaltrust.org.uk/main/w-vh/w-visits/
w-findaplace/w-comptoncastle.htm
A National Trust property since 1951, Compton Castle is a medieval fortified manor house complete with curtain walls, towers and portcullis gates. For most of its history this has been the home of the Gilbert family, including the Elizabethan explorer Sir Humphrey Gilbert, famous as the coloniser of Newfoundland in 1583 and half-brother to Sir Walter Raleigh. Enclosed within outer walls are rose, knot and herb gardens.

Cookworthy Museum   2B 34

108 Fore Street, Kingsbridge TQ7 1AW.
Tel: 01548 853235.
www.kingsbridgemuseum.org.uk
Explains the history of Kingsbridge through its collection of artifacts, costume and photographs. Founded in 1971 in the old Kingsbridge Grammar School buildings the Museum is named after William Cookworthy, who was born in Kingsbridge. In the mid 18th century Cookworthy discovered China Clay in Cornwall and developed a way to process it into fine porcelain, which had previously needed to be imported from China. Clay extraction went on to become a major Cornish industry.

Dartmoor Otter Sanctuary

see Buckfast Butterflies.

Dartmouth Museum   1B 30

The Butterwalk, Duke Street TQ6 9PZ.
Tel: 01803 832923.
www.dartmouthmuseum.org
A small museum packed full of information about this interesting and historic town explaining its maritime, social and economic history through its collection of artefacts, models, paintings and photographs. Housed in an historic town merchants house built c.1640. King Charles II was entertained here in 1671.

Dartmouth Steam Railway   6E 23 / 4D 30

Queens Park Station, Torbay Road, Paignton TQ4 6AF. Tel: 01803 555872.
www.dartmouthrailriver.co.uk
A beautifully located steam heritage railway running from the seaside at Paignton along the spectacular coastline, through picturesque wooded countryside to the River Dart at Kingswear. A ferry boat service links to the historic town of Dartmouth.

Dawlish Museum   4D 2

The Knowle, Barton Terrace EX7 9QH.
Tel: 01626 888557.
The history of Dawlish including Victorian rooms, photographs, toys and commemorative china displays. Limited opening in summer only.

Decoy Country Park   4H 11

Decoy Road, Newton Abbot TQ12 1EB.
Tel: 01626 361101.
Centred on a former clay quarry the park features ponds, streams, fen, wet woodland and heathy woodland. The woods are home to badgers, foxes and a wide variety of bird life, while the lake and

ponds support colonies of newts, common frogs, toads and dragonflies, besides the more evident population of breeding mallards, coots and moorhens.

Golden Hind
2E **29**

The Quay, Brixham Harbour TQ5 8AW.
Tel: 01803 856223.
www.goldenhind.co.uk
A full size reconstruction of the Golden Hind in which Sir Francis Drake circumnavigated the world between 1577 and 1580, returning with a valuable cargo of treasure. Drake was knighted onboard by Queen Elizabeth Ist. The replica offers a unique insight into life aboard a 16th century sailing ship, its five decks home to 70 crew living in cramped and primitive conditions.

Greenway
5B **26**

Greenway Road, Galmpton, Brixham TQ5 0ES.
Tel: 01803 842382.
www.nationaltrust.org.uk/main/w-visits/w-findaplace/w-greenway/
Agatha Christie's family holiday home has recently been opened to the public by the National Trust. It is furnished in the 1950s period and contains personal memorabilia. The large woodland garden extends to the bank of the River Dart. There are ferries from Dittisham, Dartmouth, Totnes and Torquay to Greenway Quay.

Beach Huts at Paignton

© Jennifer Thompson, image from BigStockPhoto.com

Homeyards Botanical Gardens
6C **8**

Torquay Road, Shaldon TQ14 0AY.
www.shaldon-village.co.uk/homeyards.html
A terraced arboretum on a steeply sloping site above the picturesque village of Shaldon, featuring Italian, pond and rill gardens, with lovely views over the River Teign estuary. Created by Maria Homeyard with the fortune made by her husband, the inventor and manufacturer of Liqufruta.

House of Marbles
5C **4**

Teign Valley Glass,
The Old Pottery, Pottery Road,
Bovey Tracy TQ13 9DS.
Tel: 01626 835285.
www.houseofmarbles.com
There is a museum of glass, pottery, games and a collection of marble runs at this working glass & games factory.

Kent's Cavern
4F **21**

91 Ilsham Road, Torquay TQ1 2JF.
Tel: 01803 215136.
www.kents-cavern.co.uk
Spectacular natural show caves where visitors can wonder at the displays of stalactites and stalagmites formed over millions of years. Important archaeological finds, both human and animal, show the caves were used as shelter for many thousands of years. Local families began to explore and uncover the secrets of the caves during the 18th century recovering artifacts that are amongst the earliest evidence of humans in Britain.

Kirkham House
5E **23**

Kirkham Street, Paignton TQ3 3AX.
http://www.english-heritage.org.uk/daysout/properties/kirkham-house-paignton/
A well-preserved late medieval town house, built of local stone. Now a property of English Heritage, who have furnished the rooms, with their impressive exposed timber ceilings, to suggest their original look and use.

Living Coasts
6C **20**

Torquay Harbourside, Beacon Quay TQ1 2BG.
Tel: 0844 474 3366.
www.livingcoasts.org.uk
A zoo and discovery centre which specializes in the world's coastal regions, their amazing animals and their habitats. Fish, birds and mammals are housed in specially-designed naturalistic habitats. There are both outdoor and indoor exhibits. Living Coasts is active in conservation projects in the UK and around the world.

Newcomen Engine House 1B **30** (4C **30**)

Mayor's Avenue, Dartmouth TQ6 9YY.
Tel: 01803 834224.
www.dartmouth.org.uk/Details/The-Newcomen-Engine.html
The Dartmouth engine is a memorial to Thomas Newcomen 1663-1729 born in Dartmouth, whose invention, the Atmospheric Steam Engine, was an important advance in the development of industrial technology. The engine on show is a late 18th century version, while the story of Newcomen and his inventions is displayed on interpretive panels.

Newton Abbot Town and GWR Museum 2H **11**

2a St Pauls Road TQ12 2HP.
Tel: 01626 201121.
www.museum-newtonabbot.co.uk
Displays illustrate the history of Newton Abbot from ancient to modern times, the history of the Great Western Railway and the life and achievements of its designer, Isambard Kingdom Brunel.

Oldway Mansion 3E **23**

Torquay Road, Paignton TQ3 2TE.
This grand house was built for Isaac Merritt Singer, founder of the sewing machine company, and later remodelled by his son Paris Singer into a mini Palace of Versailles. The mansion and its 17 acres of formal Italian gardens were bought by the local council in 1946.

Overbeck's 5E **35**

Sharpitor, Salcombe, TQ8 8LW.
Tel: 01548 842893.
www.nationaltrust.org.uk/main/w-overbecks
An exotic cliff-top garden with palms, banana trees, olive groves and wonderful views over Salcombe

Harbour. The house, built by Otto Overbeck, is now a museum to display his eccentric collections.

Paignton & Dartmouth Steam Railway

see Dartmouth Steam Railway.

Paignton Zoo 1C **24**

Totnes Road TQ4 7EU. Tel: 01803 697 500.
www.paigntonzoo.org.uk
With some three thousand animals distributed over five different habitats Paignton Zoo invites you to an exciting and informative wildlife experience. Have fun seeing the 'big cats', gorillas, monkeys, elephants, giraffes, rhinocerouses, crocodiles, snakes, birds and small mammals. Many of the species are managed in captivity as part of breeding programmes, the zoo being dedicated to conserving the global wildlife heritage.

Salcombe Maritime and Local History Museum 2H **35**

Town Hall Basement, Market Street TQ8 8DE.
Displaying models, ships logs, historical paintings and photographs, the museum illustrates the community's long association with the sea. With exhibitions changing annually, themes include shipbuilding, smuggling and shipwrecks.

Shaldon Wildlife Trust 6D **8**

Ness Drive TQ14 0HP. Tel: 01626 872234.
www.shaldonwildlifetrust.org.uk
This small zoo is set in an acre of woodland and sub-tropical gardens on the Ness Headland. Its specialisation is a collection of small mammals and it is recognised for its work on the conservation of critically endangered primates.

Oldway Mansion

South Devon Railway
2F **31** / 4D **32**

The Station, Dart Bridge Road, Buckfastleigh,
TQ11 0DZ. Tel: 0845 345 1420.
www.southdevonrailway.co.uk
This seven mile heritage steam railway winds it way
through the beautiful River Dart valley linking
Buckfastleigh and Totnes with an intermediate stop at
Staverton. At Buckfastleigh station the South Devon
Railway Museum tells the story of the line from its
Great Western Railway beginnings to today; displays
include the only surviving broad gauge locomotive.
The railway has a large collection of historic
locomotives and rolling stock.

Stover Country Park
5F **5**

Stover, Newton Abbot TQ12 6QG.
Tel: 01626 835236.
www.devon.gov.uk/stover_country_park.htm
This country park extends over 114 acres and
encompasses a wide range of easily accessible
habitat types, including freshwater, marshland,
coniferous and broadleaved woodlands, lowland
heath and grassland. The lake supports many bird
species and also a number of rare dragonflies. The
park features an aerial walkway through the lower
canopy of the woodland that gives visitors a bird's
eye view of the woodland and ponds below. A Nature
Interpretation Centre has interactive displays
explaining many aspects of the environment, wildlife,
geography and history of the park.

Teign Heritage Centre
4E **9**

29 French Street TQ14 8ST. Tel: 01626 777041.
www.teignheritage.org.uk
Housed in a new showcase building the museum
displays local history from prehistoric times to the
present. It explains the importance of the shipbuilding
industry and, following the building of the railway, the
transformation of Teignmouth as it became one of the
early fashionable seaside resorts.

Torquay Museum
5D **20**

529 Babbacombe Road TQ1 1HG.
Tel: 01803 293975.
www.torquaymuseum.org
The museum was founded in 1844 by the Torquay
Natural History Society and now has displays
covering not only natural history but also
palaeontology, archaeology, social history and
ethnography relating to Torbay and beyond. The
Explorers and Egyptomania gallery forms the
centrepiece of the museum, while other features
include a fully equipped life size reconstruction of an
1860's Devon farmhouse complete with sounds and
smells, a gallery dedicated to Agatha Christie and a
Torquay pottery collection.

© Jennifer Thompson. image from BigStockPhoto.com

Torre Abbey

Torre Abbey
5A **20**

The King's Drive, Torquay TQ2 5JE.
Tel: 01803 293 593.
www.torre-abbey.org.uk
Founded in 1196 Torre Abbey had become the
wealthiest Premonstratensian Abbey in England by
the close of the 15th century. Following the
Dissolution of the Monasteries, the buildings were
bought by the Cary family in 1662 and remained a
private house until 1930, when it was purchased by
the local authority for use as an art gallery. The fine
18th century galleries display landscape and marine
paintings by British artists, and feature Pre-
Raphaelite works of national standing by Holman
Hunt, Edward Burne-Jones and William Blake. Other
features of note include the medieval undercroft, the
Palm House in the Abbey Gardens, ruins of the
former medieval abbey church and a medieval Tithe
Barn, built to store taxes paid to the Abbey in the
form of farm produce.

Totnes Castle
3E **31**

Castle Street TQ9 5NU.
Tel: 01803 864406.
www.english-heritage.org.uk/daysout/properties/
totnes-castle/
Dominating the town skyline, this is a text-book
Norman motte and bailey castle and features an
impressive stone medieval keep. A walk around the
battlements affords panoramic views over the town
and surrounding countryside.

© Sam Rosbottom. image from BigStockPhoto.com

Totnes Elizabethan House Museum   4F 31

70 Fore Street TQ9 5RU.
Tel: 01803 863821.
www.devonmuseums.net/
This Elizabethan Merchant's House, built around
1575, houses Totnes Museum. Its rooms, spread over
three floors, display some 5,000 years of history from
Totnes and its District. Features include an
Elizabethan Forehall, with examples of Elizabethan
and Jacobean furniture, and the Tudor Kitchen which
compares food and cookery through both the
Elizabethan and Victorian periods.

There is a room dedicated to Victorian mechanical
computer inventor Charles Babbage who attended
the Grammar School in Totnes.

Valiant Soldier Museum   4C 32

76 Fore Street, Buckfastleigh TQ11 0BS.
Tel: 01364 644522.
www.valiantsoldier.org.uk
The Valiant Soldier public house is a time capsule,
untouched since its closure in 1965. Experience a
public house as it was fifty years ago as well as the
living quarters of the landlord and a treasure trove of
objects from a bygone age.